THE MYSTERY OF THE HELL BOUND TICKET

David S. Philemon

Royal Diadem Publishing Inc.

The Mystery of the Hell Bound Ticket
978-1-966141-42-6

For permissions, additional information, or bulk order inquiries, please
contact the author.

Write:
Royal Diadem Publishing Inc.
4836 W. 13th Street, Cicero, IL 60804
1 (312) 970 0183

Unless otherwise indicated, all Scripture quotations in this
volume are taken from the King James Version (KJV) and the
New King James Version (NKJV) of the Holy Bible.

ACKNOWLEDGMENTS

This book would not have been possible without the unwavering support, dedication, and talent of an extraordinary team. My deepest gratitude goes to each of you for your contributions, insights, and encouragement throughout this journey.

First and foremost, thank you to Rev. Mimi Philemon my dear wife, Rev. Shina Gentry, and and my assistant pastor Rev. Bright Amudoaghan for your incredible effort, encouragement, and belief in this project. Your support has been instrumental in bringing this vision to life.

To the dedicated leaders of Royal Diadem Publishing, Ide Imogie and Kishawna Bailey, I am immensely grateful for your belief in this project from the very beginning and for investing your time and energy into its development. Your creativity, dedication, and expertise have been the backbone of this endeavor.

I am especially grateful to the Royal Diadem Publishing team—Beulah Orogun, Emmanuella Ben-Eboh, Doyinsade Awodele, Kim Matthews, and Shante Gill, for your meticulous attention to detail, refining every page and ensuring that each word reflects our vision.

A heartfelt thank you to my family, friends, and colleagues whose unwavering support and belief in this project gave me the courage and strength to see it through.

Finally, thank you to all the readers and supporters who make this work meaningful. I am humbled and honored to share this journey with each of you.

With all my gratitude,
David Philemon

CONTENTS

FROM APOSTLE DR. DAVID PHILEMON

INTRODUCTION

L ife is a journey, and with every journey comes a ticket. Spiritually, the concept of a "ticket" isn't just a metaphor; it represents the path and destination our souls are on. Many are unaware that the choices they make, the influences they embrace, and the spiritual forces they engage with are stamping their ticket to a final destination—either heaven or hell.

But what is this "Hell Bound Ticket"? Simply put, it is the spiritual agreement and pathway that leads a person away from God's plan and into eternal separation from Him. Unlike a physical ticket, which can be seen and held, this spiritual ticket is often invisible to the naked eye. Yet, it is very real, guiding the course of many lives without them even realizing it.

This book probes deep into the mystery behind the Hell Bound Ticket. We will explore how people unknowingly receive these tickets, the role of sin and spiritual deception in binding people to this path, and, most importantly, how to cancel these tickets and turn toward the life God has destined for us.

As believers, it is critical that we understand the nature of this battle. The enemy does not rest, he constantly seeks to lure people onto the path of destruction. Through distractions, temptations, and subtle spiritual attacks, he attempts to issue Hell Bound Tickets, ensuring that people remain bound in sin, confusion, and spiritual blindness.

But there is good news. Just as there is a Hell Bound Ticket, there is also a way out, a spiritual return ticket to God's mercy, grace, and ultimate salvation. This book will guide you through the steps to recognize when your life is heading down the wrong path and how to invoke the power of God to break free.

The purpose of this book is not to condemn but to enlighten. Many people are spiritually unaware of the forces at play in their lives. They are sincere in their faith but fall prey to the traps of the enemy. Through the revelations shared here, I aim to expose the hidden works of the enemy and equip you with the knowledge and tools to fight back.

By the end of this book, you will not only understand the danger of holding onto a Hell Bound Ticket but also the divine strategies for canceling it. You will learn how to invoke God's covenant of mercy, stand firm in your faith, and walk in spiritual victory, free from the entrapments of the enemy.

Get ready because this is more than just a teaching; it's a spiritual awakening. It's time to cancel every Hell Bound Ticket in your life and embrace the divine path God has prepared for you.

CHAPTER ONE

UNDERSTANDING
SPIRITUAL TICKETS

What a "Ticket" Represents Spiritually

Daily, we encounter various tickets that grant us access to different experiences, be it a concert, a flight, or a sporting event. These tickets serve as a tangible representation of our rights to participate in specific events or journeys. Spiritually, the concept of a "ticket" transcends this simple analogy, embodying the deeper realities of our faith, choices, and, ultimately, our eternal destinies.

The idea of a spiritual ticket can be likened to our standing before God and the choices we make throughout our lives. Just as a ticket determines our entry into certain physical realms, spiritual tickets dictate our access to blessings, protection, and, ultimately, salvation. This chapter will explore what a spiritual ticket represents, how we acquire it, and its implications on our spiritual journeys.

The Nature of Spiritual Tickets

A spiritual ticket represents our connection to God and the spiritual realm. When we make decisions aligned with God's will, we can be seen as holding a ticket that grants us access to His promises and blessings. On the other hand, when we make choices contrary to His guidance, we may unwittingly accept a ticket that leads to spiritual destruction.

In the Bible, the idea of tickets can be illustrated through various scriptures. For example, in John 3:16, we are reminded, "For God so loved the world that He gave His only begotten Son, that whoever believes in Him should not perish but have everlasting life." This verse is an invitation, or a "ticket," to eternal life through faith in Jesus Christ. Accepting this ticket signifies our commitment to live by God's principles, granting us entry into a life marked by peace, hope, and purpose.

On the other hand, the Bible also warns us about the consequences of our choices. In Matthew 7:13-14, Jesus speaks of two paths: "Enter by the narrow gate; for wide is the gate and broad is the way that leads to destruction, and many go in by it. Because narrow is the gate and difficult is the way which leads to life, and few find it." Here, the narrow gate represents a ticket to life and righteousness, while the wide gate symbolizes a ticket to destruction. Each choice we make either reinforces our commitment to the narrow path or leads us further along the wide path, which ultimately leads to spiritual death.

The Journey of Acquiring Spiritual Tickets

Just as physical tickets must be purchased or earned, spiritual tickets require intentional decisions and commitments. The journey of acquiring a spiritual ticket begins with accepting Jesus Christ as our Lord and Savior. This foundational step opens the door to all other spiritual blessings. As we confess our sins and invite Jesus into our lives, we receive our first spiritual ticket, granting us access to eternal life and a relationship with God.

However, receiving this ticket is just the beginning. As believers, we must actively engage in our faith, making choices that align with God's Word and purpose. This involves daily acts of obedience, seeking God in prayer, studying the Scriptures, and participating in the church's life. These actions strengthen our connection to God and reinforce our standing as ticket-holders in His kingdom.

Moreover, our choices throughout our lives determine whether our spiritual tickets remain valid or void. Acts of disobedience, sin, and neglect of our relationship with God can tarnish or invalidate our spiritual tickets. For instance, in Galatians 5:19-21, Paul outlines the works of the flesh, warning that those who practice such things will not inherit the kingdom of God. This serves as a stark reminder that our actions have consequences in the spiritual realm.

The Power of Faith in Holding Our Spiritual Tickets

A significant aspect of understanding spiritual tickets is recognizing the role of faith in sustaining them. Our faith is the anchor that keeps us connected to God and His promises. Hebrews 11:1 defines faith as "the substance of things hoped for, the evidence of things not seen." When we hold onto our spiritual tickets with faith, we trust God's character and ability to fulfill His promises, even when circumstances seem contrary.

It is essential to understand that faith is not a passive state of being; it requires action. Just as a physical ticket must be presented to gain entry, our faith must be expressed through our actions and choices. James 2:17 emphasizes this point, stating, "Thus also faith by itself, if it does not have works, is dead." This means that our faith must be accompanied by corresponding actions that reflect our commitment to God.

When we actively engage our faith, we are better equipped to navigate the challenges and distractions that seek to divert us from our spiritual paths. In times of difficulty, our faith reminds us of the truth of God's word and the validity of our spiritual tickets. It empowers us to stand firm against the lies of the enemy and the temptations that threaten to lead us astray.

The Consequences of Misplaced Spiritual Tickets

Understanding spiritual tickets also necessitates recognizing the consequences of misplacing or mishandling them. Just as a lost or expired physical ticket can result in denied access, a misplaced spiritual ticket can lead to severe spiritual repercussions. When we neglect our relationship with God, we risk allowing the enemy to hand us a Hell-Bound Ticket—one that leads to destruction and separation from God's grace.

The enemy's primary goal is to divert our attention away from God, causing us to accept spiritual tickets that lead us away from His promises. In 1 Peter 5:8, we are cautioned to "be sober, be vigilant; because your adversary the devil walks about like a roaring lion, seeking whom he may devour." This warning signifies the importance of vigilance in our spiritual journey. If we are not careful, we may unknowingly accept a ticket that leads us away from God's will.

Additionally, when we engage in sinful behavior or embrace a lifestyle contrary to God's Word, we inadvertently relinquish the blessings and access that come with our spiritual tickets. Just as a physical ticket can become invalidated through misuse or negligence, our spiritual tickets can become compromised when we live outside God's standards. This is why we must remain steadfast in our commitment to God and His ways.

Reclaiming and Validating Our Spiritual Tickets

The good news is that even if we hold a Hell Bound Ticket, we can reclaim our spiritual standing. Through repentance and returning to God, we can validate our spiritual tickets again. In 1 John 1:9, we are assured, "If we confess our sins, He is faithful and just to forgive us our sins and to cleanse us from all unrighteousness." This promise emphasizes the power of confession and repentance in restoring our relationship with God.

We must first acknowledge the choices that have led us astray to reclaim our spiritual tickets. This requires honesty and humility before God. Once we recognize our missteps, we can actively seek His forgiveness and guidance to return to the narrow path that leads to life.

In addition to repentance, we must take proactive measures to protect our spiritual tickets. This includes surrounding ourselves with fellow believers who can encourage us, hold us accountable in our spiritual walks, and continually seek God's presence in our lives. The community of faith serves as a vital support system that can help us navigate challenges and stay committed to our spiritual journeys.

As we understand what spiritual tickets represent, we gain the insight to navigate our spiritual lives effectively. By actively engaging with our faith and making intentional choices, we can ensure that our spiritual tickets remain valid, granting us access to the abundant life that God promises.

Lastly, understanding what a spiritual ticket represents is crucial for every believer navigating the complexities of faith and choices. By recognizing the power of our decisions and the role of faith, we can confidently hold onto our spiritual tickets, ensuring that we remain on the path that leads to eternal life.

How People Unknowingly Accept a "Hell-Bound" Ticket
As we continue our exploration of spiritual tickets, it is crucial to understand how many individuals unknowingly accept a Hell Bound Ticket. This ticket leads them away from God's promises and into a life of spiritual destruction. The enemy is cunning and deceptive, often using subtle tactics to divert our attention and lead us down a path that contradicts God's purpose for our lives. This part will examine how people can accept this ticket, the signs to watch for it, and the importance of remaining vigilant in our spiritual journeys.

The Influence of Culture and Society

One of the primary ways individuals unknowingly accept a Hell Bound Ticket is through the pervasive influence of culture and society. We live in a world that often promotes values and ideologies contrary to biblical principles. The media, entertainment, and popular culture frequently glorify behaviors that lead to spiritual decay, enticing individuals to conform to worldly standards rather than God's.

In Romans 12:2, Paul admonishes believers, "And do not be conformed to this world, but be transformed by the renewing of your mind." This verse highlights the importance of resisting cultural pressures that seek to shape our beliefs and behaviors. Unfortunately, many people succumb to these influences, inadvertently accepting a ticket that distances them from God's truth. They may begin to adopt lifestyles, relationships, or practices that do not align with their faith, thus opening the door to spiritual compromise.

For instance, consider the normalization of behaviors such as premarital sex, substance abuse, and dishonesty in many societies today. Individuals may feel pressured to engage in these activities to fit in or seek peer acceptance. In doing so, they may not realize that they are straying from God's design for their lives, effectively accepting a Hell Bound Ticket that leads to destruction.

Ignoring the Warning Signs

Another way people unknowingly accept a Hell Bound Ticket is by ignoring the warning signs that God provides. Throughout Scripture, God has guided us on how to live righteously. However, when we become desensitized to His voice or ignore His promptings, we open ourselves up to deception.
The Holy Spirit serves as our helper and guide, continually reminding us of God's truth and prompting us to make righteous choices. However, many people choose to silence this still, small voice within them. In doing so, they risk taking steps that lead them further away from God and into danger.

For example, an individual may feel uneasy about a particular relationship or decision but ignore those feelings, convincing themselves that everything will work out. This disregard for God's warnings can lead to choices that ultimately result in spiritual harm. In Proverbs 14:12, we are reminded, "There is a way that seems right to a man, but its end is the way of death." Ignoring the warning signs, we risk walking down paths that may appear harmless but lead to destruction.

The Power of Deceptive Teachings

In recent years, we have seen a rise in deceptive teachings that distort the truth of the Gospel. False prophets and teachers often emerge, leading believers astray with teachings that cater to their desires rather than God's Word. These teachings may focus on prosperity, self-gratification, and personal happiness, neglecting the call to repentance, holiness, and obedience.

Many unknowingly accept a Hell Bound Ticket by embracing these false teachings, believing they are on the right path. They may become enamored with the promises of success and happiness, neglecting the foundational truths of Scripture that warn against sin and compromise.

Jesus warned of these deceptive influences in Matthew 7:15, saying, "Beware of false prophets, who come to you in sheep's clothing, but inwardly they are ravenous wolves." This warning reminds us that not everything that appears good is aligned with God's will. Believers must remain discerning and grounded in the truth of God's Word to avoid being led astray by misleading teachings.

Compromise in Relationships

Our relationships can significantly impact our spiritual journeys. Many individuals unknowingly accept a Hell Bound Ticket through their associations with those who do not share their faith. The people we surround ourselves with can influence our beliefs, values, and behaviors, often leading us toward compromise.

1 Corinthians 15:33 warns, "Do not be deceived: 'Evil company corrupts good habits.'" When we engage in close relationships with individuals who do not uphold biblical values, we risk adopting their perspectives and behaviors. This can lead to a gradual erosion of our faith and convictions, ultimately resulting in the acceptance of a Hell Bound Ticket.

For instance, a young believer may be drawn into a friendship with someone engaging in sinful behaviors. Initially, they may maintain their faith, but over time, they may compromise their values to keep the relationship. This can lead to a downward spiral, where their faith is undermined, and they unknowingly accept a ticket that leads them away from God's purpose.

Spiritual Laziness and Apathy

Spiritual laziness and apathy are significant contributors to the acceptance of a Hell-bound ticket. In today's fast-paced world, it is easy for individuals to become complacent in their spiritual lives. They may neglect prayer, Bible study, and church participation, leading to a weakened faith and vulnerability to the enemy's attacks.

Hebrews 2:1 urges us to "give the more earnest heed to the things we have heard, lest we drift away." This verse emphasizes the importance of remaining attentive and proactive in spiritual life. When we become lax in our faith, we risk drifting away from the truth and unknowingly accepting a ticket that leads to destruction.

A lack of spiritual discipline can lead to a spiritual drought, where individuals feel distant from God and lose sight of His promises. In such moments, the enemy can easily exploit their vulnerability, leading them to accept a Hell Bound Ticket through distractions, temptations, or doubts.

Allowing Bitterness and Unforgiveness to Take Root

Bitterness and unforgiveness can also act as gateways for accepting a Hell Bound Ticket. When individuals harbor resentment or refuse to forgive others, they create a spiritual stronghold that allows the enemy to gain a foothold in their lives. The bitterness they hold onto can cloud their judgment, leading them to make choices that distance them from God's grace.

Ephesians 4:31-32 instructs us to "let all bitterness, wrath, anger, clamor, and evil speaking be put away from you, with all malice. And be kind to one another, tenderhearted, forgiving one another, even as God in Christ forgave you." This passage reminds us of the importance of letting go of negative emotions and extending forgiveness to others. When we choose to harbor bitterness, we risk accepting a ticket that leads to spiritual stagnation and decay.

Unforgiveness can also prevent us from experiencing God's grace and mercy. When we refuse to forgive others, we create barriers between ourselves and God, hindering our spiritual growth. This can lead to feelings of guilt, shame, and separation from God, ultimately resulting in the acceptance of a Hell Bound Ticket.

The Danger of Complacency in Faith

Finally, complacency in faith can lead to accepting a Hell Bound Ticket. Many individuals start their spiritual journeys with enthusiasm and passion for God. However, as they encounter challenges and disappointments over time, they may become complacent, settling into a routine lacking enthusiasm and commitment.

Revelation 3:15-16 warns against complacency, stating, "I know your works, that you are neither cold nor hot. I could wish you were cold or hot. So then, because you are lukewarm and neither cold nor hot, I will vomit you out of My mouth." This verse emphasizes God's disdain for complacency and the danger of living a lukewarm faith.

When believers become complacent, they risk becoming indifferent to God's things, neglecting their spiritual responsibilities, and losing sight of their purpose. This complacency can lead to spiritual apathy, making it easier for the enemy to introduce a Hell-Bound Ticket into their lives.

Understanding how people unknowingly accept a Hell Bound Ticket is crucial for every believer. By remaining vigilant against cultural influences, ignoring warning signs, embracing deceptive teachings, evaluating our relationships, combating spiritual laziness, letting go of bitterness, and avoiding complacency, we can protect ourselves from the pitfalls that lead to destruction.

CHAPTER TWO

THE ROLE OF SIN IN ACQUIRING HELL-BOUND TICKET

How Sin and Disobedience Lead People Down This Path

I n exploring spiritual tickets, it becomes increasingly evident that sin plays a central role in acquiring a Hell Bound Ticket. The concept of sin is multifaceted, encompassing actions, thoughts, and attitudes that defy God's laws and principles. Disobedience to God's word creates a separation from Him, leading individuals down paths that ultimately result in spiritual destruction. Let's look into the nature of sin, its consequences, and how it manifests in our lives, guiding us toward acceptance of a Hell Bound Ticket.

Understanding Sin: A Biblical Perspective

To grasp the significance of sin in our spiritual journeys, we must first understand what sin is from a biblical perspective. Sin is any action, thought, or behavior that goes against God's commandments and moral standards. In 1 John 3:4, Apostle John provides a succinct definition: "Whoever sins also commits lawlessness, and sin is lawlessness." This verse emphasizes that sin is not merely a mistake or a lapse in judgment but a willful act of rebellion against God's authority.

The origins of sin can be traced back to the Garden of Eden, where Adam and Eve chose to disobey God's command by eating from the tree of the knowledge of good and evil (Genesis 3:6). This act of disobedience ushered sin into the world, resulting in a separation between humanity and God. The consequences of this choice were severe: not only did it lead to spiritual death, but it also set a precedent for all humanity to grapple with the reality of sin.

The Consequences of Sin

Sin has far-reaching consequences that affect our spiritual lives and our relationship with God. It impacts us emotionally and mentally and significantly influences our spiritual well-being, distancing us from the fullness of life that God intended for us. To understand the gravity of sin, we must first acknowledge that it disrupts our communion with God and causes a ripple effect in other areas of life.

Spiritual Separation from God: One of the most immediate effects of sin is spiritual separation from God. This separation is not merely a temporary disconnection but a severe breach of the relationship between humanity and its Creator. Isaiah 59:2 clarifies: "But your iniquities have separated you from your God; and your sins have hidden His face from you so that He will not hear." This scripture emphasizes that sin creates a barrier between us and God. When we engage in sinful actions, thoughts, or attitudes, we effectively sever the intimate connection we are meant to enjoy with God. The sense of closeness and divine fellowship becomes disrupted, and as a result, we often feel distant from God's presence and guidance.

The Bible repeatedly affirms that God is holy, and in His holiness, He cannot tolerate sin. Habakkuk 1:13 states, "Your eyes are too pure to look on evil; you cannot tolerate wrongdoing." When sin, we knowingly or unknowingly turn away from God's holiness. The consequence of this separation is a broken relationship and a gradual hardening of the heart. The more we sin, the more we drift from God, making it increasingly difficult to return to Him because the sensitivity to His Spirit diminishes.

Sin is, at its foundation, rebellion against God's authority and His righteous standards. When we choose to sin, we choose to step outside of God's protective boundaries. This act of rebellion places us at odds with God's will, and as Romans 6:23 warns, "The wages of sin is death." This death is not merely physical but also spiritual —eternal separation from God's presence. It is this spiritual death that manifests through the disconnection and disintegration of our relationship with the divine.

Guilt and Shame: The Internal Consequence of Sin: In addition to the spiritual separation that sin causes, there are internal emotional and psychological effects, particularly guilt and shame. After indulging in sinful behavior, individuals often experience a cycle of remorse and regret. Initially, sin may offer a fleeting sense of pleasure or satisfaction. However, this feeling is quickly followed by an overwhelming sense of guilt as the Holy Spirit convicts us of our wrongdoing.

Guilt, when left unaddressed, festers and turns into shame. Shame is more profound and more personal, it is not just a feeling that we have done something wrong; it becomes a sense of unworthiness. Shame causes us to withdraw from God, from others, and from ourselves. Genesis 3:8-10 illustrates this vividly in the story of Adam and Eve. After they sinned, they hid from God, ashamed of their nakedness and afraid to confront Him. This reflects what many believers experience when they fall into sin. The fear of judgment, the weight of guilt, and the internal turmoil all push us away from seeking God's presence.

The enemy, Satan, capitalizes on these feelings of guilt and shame. He uses them as tools to drive us further away from God, whispering lies that we are beyond forgiveness or that we are too sinful to be accepted back into God's grace. This is one of the most dangerous consequences of sin: it leads us to believe we are unworthy of redemption. Revelation 12:10 refers to Satan as "the accuser of the brethren," constantly accusing and reminding believers of their failures, thus keeping them bound in guilt.

This cycle of guilt and shame also hinders spiritual growth. Instead of growing in the knowledge and love of God, we become stagnant, paralyzed by our sins. When guilt becomes a permanent fixture in our hearts, we stop seeking God for guidance, comfort, and forgiveness. This stagnation stifles the fruit of the Spirit in our lives, making it difficult for us to bear love, joy, peace, and self-control, qualities that are essential for a vibrant and fulfilling spiritual life.

The Long-Term Effects of Sin: Beyond the immediate spiritual and emotional consequences, sin has long-term repercussions that affect every aspect of our lives. If left unchecked, sin can evolve from occasional lapses into entrenched patterns of behavior, leading to a hardened heart. Hebrews 3:13 warns believers to "encourage one another daily, as long as it is called 'Today,' so that sin's deceitfulness may harden none of you." Sin, especially when indulged in regularly, can dull our sensitivity to the voice of the Holy Spirit and distort our moral compass.

As sin hardens the heart, it becomes increasingly difficult for individuals to recognize their need for repentance. This leads to a dangerous place where people become comfortable in their sin, justifying their behavior or ignoring the conviction of the Holy Spirit. Over time, the ability to discern right from wrong becomes blurred, and individuals fall deeper into sinful habits. 1 Timothy 4:2 refers to those whose "consciences have been seared as with a hot iron," meaning they have become desensitized to the conviction of sin.

The long-term consequence of sin also extends to our

relationships with others. Sin often leads to brokenness in relationships, whether through lies, infidelity, anger, or selfishness. As we distance ourselves from God, we lose the ability to reflect His love and grace to others. As a result, relationships suffer, marred by conflict, distrust, and bitterness. James 4:1-2 speaks to this, saying, "What causes fights and quarrels among you? Don't they come from your desires that battle within you? You desire but do not have, so you kill. You covet but you cannot get what you want, so you quarrel and fight." The internal struggles caused by sin manifest externally in how we treat those around us.

Sin's Deceptive Nature and Its Impact on Purpose: Another insidious aspect of sin is its deceptive nature. Sin often presents itself as something harmless or desirable, making it easy for individuals to fall into its trap. James 1:14-15 explains this process: "But each person is tempted when they are dragged away by their evil desire and enticed. Then, after desire has conceived, it gives birth to sin; and sin, when it is full-grown, gives birth to death." Sin rarely appears as dangerous at first glance. It entices through momentary pleasure, false promises, or the desire to fulfill immediate needs. However, once it takes root, it grows and eventually leads to spiritual death.

The enemy often presents sin as something enticing and harmless, convincing individuals that it will bring them fulfillment or happiness. In Genesis 3:6, we see how the serpent deceived Eve, appealing to her desires and presenting the forbidden fruit as something that would enhance her life: "So when the woman saw that the tree was good for food, that it was pleasant to the eyes, and a tree desirable to make one wise, she took of its fruit and ate." This moment of deception led to catastrophic consequences, demonstrating how sin can appear alluring while leading to destruction.

In modern society, this deception persists. Many individuals are lured into sinful behaviors by the allure of instant gratification, societal acceptance, or the belief that they are missing out on something enjoyable. The enemy capitalizes on these desires, blinding individuals to the reality of the spiritual consequences that await them. The allure of sin can be particularly potent in a culture that celebrates rebellion against God's standards, leading many to accept a Hell Bound Ticket without even realizing it.

This deception also impacts the fulfillment of God's purpose in our lives. Each of us has been created with a unique purpose and calling, but sin disrupts our ability to walk in that purpose. When we live in sin, we distance ourselves from the very source of our purpose—God. Jeremiah 29:11 tells us that God has plans to prosper and give us hope, but sin veils our ability to see or pursue those plans. Instead of walking in God's purpose, we become distracted, pursuing temporary satisfaction rather than eternal significance.

The enemy knows that sin diminishes our ability to fulfill God's purpose. By keeping us bound in sin, he can prevent us from being effective witnesses for Christ. Matthew 5:14-16 calls believers to be the light of the world, shining brightly in a dark world. However, when sin overtakes our lives, our light dims, and our testimony becomes compromised. We lose the ability to be examples of God's transforming power, and our effectiveness in spreading the Gospel is hindered.

The Remedy: Repentance and God's Mercy: Despite the devastating consequences of sin, there is hope. God, in His infinite mercy, has provided a way for us to be free from the bondage of sin. The remedy for sin is repentance—a turning away from sinful behaviors and returning to God's grace. 1 John 1:9 says, "If we confess our sins, He is faithful and just to forgive us our sins and cleanse us from all unrighteousness." This is the good news of the Gospel: no matter how far we have fallen, God's mercy is always available to restore us.

Repentance is not merely feeling sorry for our sins but a

complete change of heart and mind. It involves recognizing the seriousness of sin, acknowledging its impact on our relationship with God, and choosing to turn away from it. True repentance is accompanied by humility, as we admit that we cannot overcome sin alone but need God's grace and strength to lead us into freedom.

Once we repent, God's forgiveness is immediate and complete. He does not hold our sins against us or remind us of our past failures. Psalm 103:12 assures us, "As far as the east is from the west, so far has He removed our transgressions from us." God's grace not only forgives but also restores, healing the brokenness caused by sin and empowering us to live in righteousness.

In addition to repentance, believers must actively pursue holiness by walking in obedience to God's word. This requires daily surrender to the Holy Spirit, allowing Him to guide our thoughts, actions, and desires. Galatians 5:16 encourages us to "walk in the Spirit, and you shall not fulfill the lust of the flesh." By aligning ourselves with the Holy Spirit, we can resist the temptations of sin and walk in the freedom that Christ has secured for us.

The Role of Disobedience in Sin

Disobedience is a critical factor in the acceptance of a Hell Bound Ticket. When we knowingly disobey God's commands, we actively reject His authority and guidance. This disobedience can take many forms, from blatant acts of rebellion to subtle compromises in our daily choices.

In Deuteronomy 30:15-16, God presents the people of Israel with a choice between life and death, blessing and cursing: "See, I have set before you today life and good, death and evil, in that I command you today to love the Lord your God, to walk in His ways, and to keep His commandments, His statutes, and His judgments, that you may live and multiply." This scripture emphasizes the importance of obedience to God's commands. When we walk in His ways, we align ourselves with His blessings. Conversely, disobedience leads to spiritual death and destruction.

The Bible is replete with examples of individuals who faced dire consequences due to disobedience. Take King Saul, for instance. Despite being chosen by God to lead Israel, Saul's disobedience led to his rejection as king. In 1 Samuel 15, Saul disobeys God's command to destroy the Amalekites and their possessions, choosing instead to spare King Agag and the best of the livestock. This disobedience resulted in God rejecting Saul as king, illustrating the severe repercussions of straying from God's commands.

The Slow Drift into Sin

Accepting a Hell Bound Ticket often occurs gradually, as individuals slowly drift into sin over time. This process can be likened to the "slippery slope" of temptation, where small compromises lead to more enormous transgressions. It is essential to recognize the warning signs of this drift to avoid falling prey to the enemy's tactics.

In James 1:14-15, we are reminded, "But each one is tempted when he is drawn away by his desires and enticed. Then, when desire has conceived, it gives birth to sin; when it is full-grown, sin brings forth death." This place emphasizes the progression from temptation to sin and the eventual consequences of unrepentant sin. When individuals allow temptation to take root in their lives without addressing it, they risk entering a cycle of sin that becomes increasingly difficult to break.

For example, consider someone who begins to engage in small acts of dishonesty, such as telling "white lies" or exaggerating their accomplishments. Initially, these actions may seem harmless, but over time, they can lead to a pattern of deceitfulness. As the individual continues down this path, they may find themselves entangled in a web of lies, ultimately leading to more significant consequences and spiritual separation from God.

The Role of Habitual Sin

Habitual sin is another significant factor that leads to the acceptance of a Hell Bound Ticket. When individuals repeatedly engage in sinful behaviors without seeking repentance, they create strongholds in their lives that can be challenging to break. These strongholds can develop into patterns of behavior that become ingrained in one's identity.

In Romans 6:16, Paul writes, "Do you not know that to whom you present yourselves slaves to obey, you are that one's slaves whom you obey, whether of sin leading to death, or of obedience leading to righteousness?" This verse highlights the idea that our choices ultimately determine our spiritual condition. When individuals habitually engage in sin, they become enslaved to that sin, effectively accepting a Hell Bound Ticket that leads to destruction.

It is essential to understand that habitual sin does not have to be a life sentence. Through the power of the Holy Spirit and the process of repentance, individuals can break free from these strongholds. However, this requires a willingness to confront the sin, seek God's forgiveness, and actively pursue a life of obedience.

The Importance of Accountability

Accountability is a critical component in combating sin and preventing the acceptance of a Hell Bound Ticket. When individuals surround themselves with a community of believers who hold them accountable, they are less likely to succumb to the temptations and distractions that lead to sin.

In Galatians 6:1-2, Paul encourages believers to "bear one another's burdens, and so fulfill the law of Christ." This call to accountability emphasizes the importance of supporting one another in our spiritual journeys. When we have trusted friends or mentors who can provide guidance and encouragement, we are better equipped to resist temptation and remain steadfast in our faith.

Also, accountability can help individuals identify areas of their lives that require repentance. Sometimes, we may not recognize the extent of our sin or its consequences until someone points it out. This is why it is crucial to cultivate relationships with fellow believers who can lovingly challenge us and help us stay on the right path.

The Need for Repentance

Repentance is an essential aspect of addressing sin and reclaiming our spiritual standing. When individuals acknowledge their wrongdoing and turn back to God, they can break free from the chains of sin and avoid accepting a Hell Bound Ticket. In Acts 3:19, we are encouraged, "Repent therefore and be converted, that your sins may be blotted out, so that times of refreshing may come from the presence of the Lord."

The act of repentance involves more than just saying "I'm sorry"; it requires a genuine desire to turn away from sin and pursue a life aligned with God's will. This process begins with recognizing the impact of our choices and the need for forgiveness. When we approach God with a contrite heart, He is faithful to cleanse us and restore our relationship with Him.

Embracing God's Grace and Mercy

As we navigate the complexities of sin and its consequences, it is essential to remember the power of God's grace and mercy. While sin can lead to spiritual destruction, God's love and forgiveness offer a path to redemption. In Romans 5:20, Paul assures us that "where sin abounded, grace abounded much more." This promise serves as a reminder that no sin is too great for God to forgive.

When individuals recognize the depth of their sin and seek God's forgiveness, they can experience a profound transformation. God's grace empowers us to break free from the chains of sin, providing the strength and courage to live in obedience. It is through this grace that we can reclaim our spiritual tickets and walk in the fullness of God's promises.

In conclusion, by understanding the nature of sin, its consequences, and the factors that lead individuals astray, we can better equip ourselves to navigate the challenges of our spiritual journeys. As we move forward, we must remain vigilant against the deceptive nature of sin, seek accountability, and embrace the power of repentance and God's grace.

Biblical Examples of Individuals on the Wrong Spiritual Path

Throughout Scripture, we find numerous examples of individuals who, through their choices, embarked on the wrong spiritual path, ultimately leading to their spiritual demise or severe consequences. These stories serve as cautionary tales, illustrating the dangers of disobedience, sin, and the acceptance of a Hell Bound Ticket. In this part, we will explore several biblical figures whose lives reflect the pitfalls of straying from God's path, highlighting their choices, the resulting consequences, and the lessons we can learn from their experiences.

Adam and Eve: The Origin of Sin

The narrative of Adam and Eve in the Garden of Eden stands as the foundational account of humanity's fall into sin. This story, found in Genesis 2 and Genesis 3, not only explains how sin entered the world but also provides deep insights into the nature of temptation, disobedience, and the consequences of rejecting God's commands. The choices made by Adam and Eve reverberate through history, affecting all of humanity and establishing a pattern of spiritual rebellion that continues to this day.

In Genesis 2:16-17, God gives a clear and simple command to Adam: "Of every tree of the garden, you may freely eat; but of the tree of the knowledge of good and evil you shall not eat, for in the day that you eat of it you shall surely die." This command is significant for several reasons. First, it reveals that God, as Creator, establishes boundaries for human behavior. These boundaries are not arbitrary but are designed for the well-being of humanity. The tree of the knowledge of good and evil represented the boundary between humanity's innocence and the knowledge of moral evil. God, in His infinite wisdom, knew that disobedience to this command would lead to spiritual death and separation from Him.

The very existence of this boundary also emphasizes the gift of free will that God gave to humanity. Unlike the rest of creation, humans were made in the image of God (Genesis 1:27) and were endowed with the capacity to make choices. This capacity for choice is essential to genuine love and relationship. Obedience to God is meaningful because it is a voluntary act of love and trust, rather than forced compliance. In the Garden, Adam and Eve were given the opportunity to choose obedience and faithfulness to God, which would have preserved their intimate fellowship with Him.

However, the command also carried a warning: "for in the day that you eat of it you shall surely die." This statement highlights the seriousness of sin. Disobedience would not only break their relationship with God but also introduce death into the human experience. This death was both spiritual and physical. Spiritually, Adam and Eve would experience separation from God, the source of life. Physically, their disobedience would eventually lead to their mortality. In essence, the command set before them life and death, with obedience leading to continued life in God's presence and disobedience leading to death and separation.

The entry of the serpent in Genesis 3 marks a turning point in the narrative. The serpent, later identified as Satan in Revelation 12:9, approaches Eve with a seemingly innocent question: "Has God indeed said, 'You shall not eat of every tree of the garden'?" (Genesis 3:1). This question, while subtle, begins the process of planting doubt in Eve's mind. Instead of directly challenging God's command, the serpent sows confusion by twisting God's words, making Eve question her understanding of what God had said.

Eve's response to the serpent in Genesis 3:2-3 indicates that she understood the command but added an additional restriction, saying, "You shall not eat it, nor shall you touch it, lest you die." This slight alteration shows that she was already beginning to drift away from the clarity of God's command. The serpent seizes this opportunity to directly contradict God's warning, stating, "You will not surely die" (Genesis 3:4). With this lie, the serpent introduces the notion that God's command was not to be trusted and that the consequences He had outlined were exaggerated.

The serpent then goes further by appealing to Eve's desire for wisdom and autonomy, saying, "For God knows that in the day you eat of it your eyes will be opened, and you will be like God, knowing good and evil" (Genesis 3:5). This statement is a mixture of truth and deception. It is true that eating the fruit would open their eyes to the knowledge of good and evil, but it is false to suggest that this would make them like God in the way the serpent implied. Instead of becoming like God in holiness and righteousness, Adam and Eve would become like God in a tragic sense, aware of evil but powerless to overcome it without divine intervention.

The serpent's tactic was to undermine Eve's trust in God's goodness and to make her believe that God was withholding something beneficial from her. This is a common tactic of the enemy, even today. He often tries to convince us that God's commands are restrictive and that true freedom and fulfillment lie outside of God's will. By focusing on the one prohibition rather than the abundance of freedom Adam and Eve had in the Garden, the serpent shifted Eve's perspective, leading her to question God's intentions.

The pivotal moment in the narrative comes in Genesis 3:6: "So when the woman saw that the tree was good for food, that it was pleasant to the eyes, and a tree desirable to make one wise, she took of its fruit and ate." This verse encapsulates the threefold nature of temptation—physical, emotional, and intellectual. Eve saw that the tree was "good for food," appealing to her physical desires. It was "pleasant to the eyes," appealing to her emotional and aesthetic senses. And it was "desirable to make one wise," appealing to her intellectual and spiritual ambitions.

This pattern of temptation is echoed in 1 John 2:16, which warns of the "lust of the flesh, the lust of the eyes, and the pride of life." These are the same tactics that the enemy uses against humanity today. Eve, drawn by the allure of these temptations, made the fateful decision to eat the fruit. Adam, who was with her, also ate the fruit, and together they disobeyed God's direct command.

The consequences of this disobedience were immediate. In Genesis 3:7, we read, "Then the eyes of both of them were opened, and they knew that they were naked." Their newfound knowledge of good and evil did not bring the wisdom and divine status they had hoped for. Instead, it brought shame and guilt. Their innocence was lost, and they could no longer stand before God without feeling exposed and vulnerable. They attempted to cover their nakedness with fig leaves, but this was merely a superficial attempt to address a much deeper problem, their broken relationship with God.

The consequences of Adam and Eve's disobedience were severe and far-reaching. The first and most devastating consequence was spiritual death, which manifested as separation from God. In Genesis 3:8, Adam and Eve "hid themselves from the presence of the Lord God among the trees of the garden." For the first time, humanity experienced fear and shame in God's presence. Instead of walking with God in the cool of the day, as they had before, they now hid from Him, knowing that their sin had created a barrier between them and their Creator.

God's question, "Where are you?" (Genesis 3:9), was not just a physical inquiry but a spiritual one. It signaled the broken relationship between God and humanity. Adam's response, "I heard Your voice in the garden, and I was afraid because I was naked; and I hid myself" (Genesis 3:10), reveals the profound impact of sin. Fear and shame replaced the openness and intimacy that Adam and Eve once enjoyed with God.

Beyond spiritual separation, physical consequences followed. God pronounced curses upon the serpent, Adam, and Eve in Genesis 3:14-19. Eve would experience pain in childbirth, and her relationship with her husband would be marked by tension. Adam would face toil and frustration in his work, as the ground itself was cursed because of his disobedience. Ultimately, both Adam and Eve were banished from the Garden of Eden, and the way to the tree of life was guarded by cherubim and a flaming sword (Genesis 3:24). This banishment symbolized the loss of eternal life and the beginning of humanity's mortal existence.

The Ripple Effect: Sin's Impact on All Humanity

Adam and Eve's disobedience did not just affect them; it affected all of humanity. Romans 5:12 explains, "Therefore, just as through one man sin entered the world, and death through sin, and thus death spread to all men, because all sinned." This verse highlights the far-reaching consequences of Adam's sin. Through his disobedience, sin and death entered the world, and every human being is born into this fallen state. The doctrine of original sin teaches that humanity is born with a sinful nature, inherited from Adam. This sinful nature separates us from God and makes us prone to rebellion and disobedience.

The Hope of Redemption: God's Plan for Restoration

Although the story of Adam and Eve's fall is tragic, it is not without hope. Even in the midst of their sin and judgment, God provides a glimmer of redemption. In Genesis 3:15, God speaks to the serpent, saying, "And I will put enmity between you and the woman, and between your seed and her Seed; He shall bruise your head, and you shall bruise His heel." This verse, often referred to as the "protoevangelium", is the first hint of the Gospel in Scripture. It foretells the coming of a Savior, the "Seed" of the woman, who would defeat Satan and bring redemption to humanity.

This promise is fulfilled in Jesus Christ, who, through His death and resurrection, conquered sin and death, providing a way for humanity to be restored to a right relationship with God. Romans 5:19 declares, "For as by one man's disobedience many were made sinners, so also by one Man's obedience many will be made righteous." Through Christ, the curse of Adam's sin is reversed, and we are offered the gift of eternal life.

The story of Adam and Eve serves as a sobering reminder of the devastating consequences of sin. It teaches us that disobedience to God leads to separation, shame, and death, while obedience leads to life and communion with Him. It also reveals the deceptive nature of sin and the importance of trusting in God's goodness and commands. However, the story also offers hope, pointing to the ultimate redemption found in Jesus Christ. Through Him, we can be freed from the consequences of sin and restored to a relationship with God.

Cain: The Consequences of Anger and Jealousy

The story of Cain and Abel, found in Genesis 4:1-16, is a powerful illustration of the destructive nature of unchecked emotions such as anger and jealousy. As the firstborn son of Adam and Eve, Cain held a significant position, yet his inability to manage his emotions led to tragic consequences. His jealousy toward his younger brother Abel, combined with unaddressed anger, culminated in the first recorded act of murder in the Bible, highlighting the catastrophic impact of allowing sin to take root in one's heart.

The conflict between Cain and Abel begins with their offerings to God. Abel, a keeper of sheep, brings a sacrificial offering from the firstborn of his flock, while Cain, a farmer, offers produce from the ground. Genesis 4:4-5 tells us, "The Lord respected Abel and his offering, but He did not respect Cain and his offering. And Cain was very angry, and his countenance fell." God's preference for Abel's offering over Cain's was not a reflection of favoritism but rather an indication of the heart condition behind the offerings. Abel's offering, given in faith and with a pure heart, was acceptable to God, while Cain's offering was rejected, possibly due to his lack of sincerity or wrong motives (Hebrews 11:4).

Cain's response to God's rejection of his offering reveals the underlying issues of his heart. Instead of seeking to understand why his offering was unacceptable and making the necessary changes, Cain allows anger and jealousy to fester. He becomes resentful of his brother's favor with God and bitter about his own perceived failure. This anger is not merely an emotional reaction; it is the beginning of a dangerous spiritual descent. Cain's failure to deal with his emotions leads him further away from God, as his focus shifts from self-reflection to comparison with his brother.

In His mercy, God offers Cain an opportunity to correct his course before it is too late. In Genesis 4:6-7, God speaks directly to Cain, asking, "Why are you angry? And why has your countenance fallen? If you do well, will you not be accepted? And if you do not do well, sin lies at the door. And its desire is for you, but you should rule over it." These verses are crucial for understanding the nature of sin and human responsibility. God is essentially telling Cain that he has a choice: he can either master his emotions and overcome the temptation to sin, or he can allow sin to master him.

The imagery of sin "lying at the door" is particularly striking. It conveys the idea that sin is always ready to pounce, waiting for an opportunity to take control. However, God's words also emphasize that Cain has the power to resist and rule over sin. This is an important reminder for all believers that while sin may be ever-present, we are not powerless in the face of temptation. God equips us with the ability to overcome sinful desires, but we must actively choose to do so.

Unfortunately, Cain disregards God's warning. Instead of confronting his anger and jealousy, he lets these emotions consume him. Rather than seeking reconciliation with God or his brother, Cain allows bitterness to fester until it manifests in violent action.

Cain's refusal to heed God's warning leads to one of the most tragic moments in Scripture—the murder of Abel. In Genesis 4:8, we read, "Now Cain talked with Abel his brother; and it came to pass, when they were in the field, that Cain rose up against Abel his brother and killed him." This verse marks the first act of murder in human history, a brother killing his own flesh and blood out of jealousy and rage.

The premeditated nature of the act is evident. Cain lures Abel into the field, away from others, and there he carries out his violent plan. It is important to note that Abel had done nothing wrong to provoke Cain's anger. Abel's only offense, if it could be called that, was his faithfulness and obedience to God, which resulted in God's favor upon him. Cain's anger was not rooted in anything Abel had done but rather in Cain's own failure to master his sinful desires.

This act of murder is symbolic of what unchecked sin can lead to when it is allowed to grow unchecked in the heart. Cain's anger, jealousy, and resentment, once fully developed, culminated in an act of irreversible destruction. This progression from internal sin to external violence serves as a warning to all believers of the dangers of allowing negative emotions to go unresolved. When we do not deal with our emotions in a healthy, God-honoring way, they can spiral out of control, leading to actions that we never imagined we were capable of.

The Consequences of Cain's Sin

The consequences of Cain's sin are immediate and severe. After the murder, God confronts Cain, asking, "Where is Abel your brother?" (Genesis 4:9). Cain's response, "I do not know. Am I my brother's keeper?" reflects both his callousness and his attempt to evade responsibility. This is a stark contrast to God's earlier warning, where He gave Cain the opportunity to master sin. Now, having committed the act, Cain's heart is hardened, and he shows no remorse or acknowledgment of his wrongdoing.

God's judgment on Cain is twofold. First, He pronounces a curse on Cain's ability to work the ground, saying, "When you till the ground, it shall no longer yield its strength to you" (Genesis 4:12). This curse strikes at the very core of Cain's identity as a farmer. His livelihood, the thing that defined him, would no longer be fruitful. This consequence mirrors the spiritual barrenness that sin brings into our lives. Just as Cain's work would no longer bear fruit, sin causes spiritual barrenness, preventing us from living in the fullness of God's blessings.

Second, God declares that Cain will be "a fugitive and a vagabond" on the earth (Genesis 4:12). This punishment is not just physical but also spiritual. Cain is condemned to a life of wandering, separated from God's presence and the community of his family. The deep loneliness and alienation that Cain experiences are the direct results of his sin. Sin always leads to isolation, both from God and from others. Just as Cain was cast out from the presence of God, sin separates us from the intimate relationship we were meant to have with our Creator.

In Genesis 4:13-14, Cain laments his punishment, saying, "My punishment is greater than I can bear! Surely You have driven me out this day from the face of the ground; I shall be hidden from Your face; I shall be a fugitive and a vagabond on the earth, and it will happen that anyone who finds me will kill me." Cain's despair reveals the true weight of his sin. He recognizes that his actions have led to complete separation from God's presence and that his life will be marked by fear, restlessness, and judgment from others.

However, even in His judgment, God shows mercy. In Genesis

4:15, the Lord says, "Therefore, whoever kills Cain, vengeance shall be taken on him sevenfold." God places a mark on Cain to protect him from being killed by others. This act of mercy shows that, despite Cain's grievous sin, God still values his life and does not allow him to be destroyed. This mirrors the way God extends mercy to all sinners, giving them opportunities to repent and turn back to Him, even after significant wrongdoing.

Lessons from Cain's Story

Cain's story serves as a powerful warning about the dangers of unchecked emotions and the consequences of allowing sin to take root in our hearts. His failure to address his anger and jealousy led to devastating outcomes, not only for Abel, who lost his life, but also for Cain, who lost his connection with God and his place in the community.

There are several important lessons we can learn from this tragic story:

The Importance of Managing Emotions: Anger and jealousy, when left unchecked, can quickly escalate into sinful actions. God's warning to Cain serves as a reminder that we must rule over our emotions rather than let them control us. Ephesians 4:26-27 tells us, "Be angry, and do not sin: do not let the sun go down on your wrath, nor give place to the devil." This verse emphasizes that while anger is a natural emotion, it must be dealt with in a healthy way to prevent it from leading to sin.

Sin's Progression: Sin often begins with small, internal attitudes, such as resentment or envy, but, if left unchecked, it grows and manifests in external actions. Cain's story shows how sin can progress from internal feelings to devastating outcomes. We must be vigilant in addressing sin at its root, before it has a chance to grow.

God's Mercy and Justice: Even in the face of Cain's grievous sin, God extends mercy by protecting his life. This demonstrates that while God is just and holds us accountable for our actions, He is also merciful and desires to give us opportunities to repent. Psalm 103:8 reminds us, "The Lord is merciful and gracious, slow to anger, and abounding in mercy."

The Consequences of Sin: Cain's life after the murder of Abel was marked by restlessness, fear, and separation from God. This illustrates the broader spiritual truth that sin leads to alienation from God and others. However, through Christ, we are offered reconciliation and the chance to restore our broken relationships with God and those around us.

Saul: The Fall of a King

King Saul's reign over Israel is a poignant and tragic example of how disobedience and pride can lead to spiritual ruin. Initially chosen by God to lead His people, Saul's story, recorded in the books of 1 Samuel, begins with great promise. He was anointed by the prophet Samuel, and the people of Israel were hopeful that Saul would lead them victoriously. However, Saul's reign takes a downward spiral due to repeated acts of disobedience, ultimately resulting in his rejection by God.

One of the most significant moments of disobedience in Saul's life is recorded in 1 Samuel 15, when God commands Saul to utterly destroy the Amalekites, a people who had long opposed Israel. God's instructions were clear: everything and everyone, including King Agag and the best of the livestock, were to be destroyed as an act of divine judgment. However, Saul fails to fully obey God's command. He spares King Agag and keeps the best of the livestock under the pretense of offering sacrifices to God.

This disobedience reveals Saul's underlying issue, his desire to prioritize his own judgment over God's. Saul's partial obedience was, in fact, complete disobedience. In 1 Samuel 15:22-23, the prophet Samuel confronts Saul, delivering a powerful rebuke:
"Has the Lord as great delight in burnt offerings and sacrifices, as in obeying the voice of the Lord? Behold, to obey is better than

sacrifice, and to heed than the fat of rams. For rebellion is as the sin of witchcraft, and stubbornness is as iniquity and idolatry."

Samuel's words reveal the seriousness of Saul's actions. God does not desire ritual sacrifices without obedience. Saul's decision to spare the best livestock for sacrifice may have seemed reasonable to him, but God values obedience far more than outward displays of religious piety.

Samuel's statement, "rebellion is as the sin of witchcraft," points to the gravity of Saul's disobedience. In God's eyes, rebellion is not a minor issue; it is akin to witchcraft, an act of defiance and separation from God's will. This passage teaches us that rebellion and stubbornness are forms of idolatry because they place human will above God's authority. Saul's disobedience was a reflection of his heart's condition, one that had drifted away from submission to God's sovereignty.

The Consequences of Saul's Pride and Disobedience

Saul's downfall can be traced back to his deep-seated insecurities and pride. Despite being chosen by God, Saul was constantly driven by fear of losing power, and this fear influenced his decisions. Rather than trusting fully in God's command, Saul's need for control and approval led him to disobey. His failure to follow God's instructions was not an isolated incident but the culmination of a pattern of insecurity and lack of faith.

Because of his disobedience, God rejected Saul as king. In 1 Samuel 15:26, Samuel declares, "You have rejected the word of the Lord, and the Lord has rejected you from being king over Israel." This rejection was not just the loss of his kingship; it marked the beginning of Saul's spiritual and emotional decline. From this point forward, Saul's reign was plagued by paranoia, insecurity, and a growing distance from God's presence. His disobedience cost him God's favor and protection, leading to the gradual erosion of his kingdom and personal peace.

One of the most significant consequences of Saul's rejection by

God was the anointing of David as the future king of Israel. 1 Samuel 16:13 describes how the Spirit of the Lord departed from Saul and rested upon David. From that moment, Saul's mental and spiritual state began to deteriorate. The Bible records that Saul was tormented by an evil spirit, and his jealousy of David, who quickly rose to prominence, became all-consuming.

The Lessons from Saul's Fall

Saul's story serves as a powerful warning about the dangers of pride and disobedience. Although he was chosen by God, Saul allowed his insecurities, fears, and pride to drive his decisions, leading him down a path of rebellion. Instead of humbling himself before God and trusting in His guidance, Saul continually sought to do things his way, convinced that his judgment was superior.

One of the most critical lessons from Saul's life is the importance of obedience to God's will. As Samuel said, "to obey is better than sacrifice." Outward religious acts or displays of devotion cannot compensate for a heart that is disobedient to God's commands. God desires submission, trust, and faithfulness. Saul's failure to obey illustrates that partial obedience is, in fact, disobedience.

In addition, Saul's story highlights the destructive power of pride. His refusal to repent and his unwillingness to accept responsibility for his actions were rooted in pride. This pride blinded him to the opportunity for reconciliation with God. Instead of turning back to God, Saul continued to spiral downward, consumed by jealousy and rage, particularly toward David, the man God chose to replace him.

The fall of King Saul is a sobering reminder that God values humility, obedience, and trust above all else. Saul's disobedience, driven by pride and insecurity, led to his rejection by God and his ultimate downfall. His story stands as a warning to all believers about the consequences of placing our own desires and judgments above God's will. Saul's life encourages us to reflect on the importance of humble submission to God's authority and to heed His commands with unwavering faithfulness. Only through humility and obedience can we walk in the fullness of God's favor and avoid the spiritual ruin that comes from rebellion.

David: A Man After God's Heart with a Dangerous Misstep

King David, known for his heart for God, is another biblical figure whose choices illustrate the consequences of sin. Despite being described as "a man after God's own heart" (1 Samuel 13:14), David's life is marked by serious moral failures, most notably in the incident involving Bathsheba.

In 2 Samuel 11, we see David's tragic fall into sin when he gazes at Bathsheba, the wife of Uriah, and desires her. Rather than fleeing temptation, David acts on his desires, committing adultery and subsequently orchestrating Uriah's death to cover up the sin. David's choices lead to significant consequences, including turmoil within his household and the eventual death of the child born from his union with Bathsheba (2 Samuel 12:14).

David's story is a powerful reminder of the importance of accountability and vigilance in our spiritual lives. Even those who are closest to God can fall into sin if they let their guard down. David's repentance, as seen in Psalm 51, showcases the path back to God after sin, emphasizing the importance of acknowledging our wrongs and seeking forgiveness.

Solomon: The Wisdom that Led to Folly

King Solomon, known for his unparalleled wisdom, also fell victim to the allure of sin. Despite receiving divine wisdom and riches, Solomon's later years were marked by disobedience. In 1 Kings 11:1-4, we read that Solomon took many foreign wives who turned his heart away from God. His marriages led him to embrace the worship of foreign gods, directly disobeying God's command not to intermarry with those outside of Israel.

The consequences of Solomon's choices were severe. His heart was turned away from the true God, and as a result, God became angry with him and announced that the kingdom would be divided after his death (1 Kings 11:9-11). Solomon's story serves as a cautionary tale about the dangers of allowing worldly influences to compromise our faith.

Solomon's example illustrates how even the wisest among us can falter when they stray from God's commandments. His life serves as a reminder of the need for diligence and the importance of surrounding ourselves with influences that uplift our faith rather than lead us astray.

Judas Iscariot: The Betrayal of Trust

Judas Iscariot, one of the twelve disciples, exemplifies the tragic consequences of greed and betrayal. Chosen by Jesus to be part of His inner circle, Judas ultimately succumbs to temptation and sells Jesus for thirty pieces of silver (Matthew 26:14-16). Despite being a witness to Jesus' miracles and teachings, Judas allows his greed to cloud his judgment.

Judas's decision to betray Jesus leads to profound consequences, both for himself and the world. After realizing the gravity of his actions, he is filled with remorse but chooses to take his own life rather than seek forgiveness (Matthew 27:3-5). Judas's story underscores the peril of allowing greed and selfish ambition to take root in our hearts, leading us away from the path of righteousness.

This narrative serves as a stark reminder of the importance of guarding our hearts against the temptation to prioritize material gain over our relationship with God. Judas's betrayal highlights how easily one can go astray, even when they are surrounded by divine truth and love.

Ananias and Sapphira: The Danger of Deception

In Acts 5:1-11, we encounter the story of Ananias and Sapphira, a couple who lied to the Holy Spirit in an attempt to deceive the early church. They sold a piece of property and kept part of the money for themselves while pretending to donate the entire amount. This act of deception led to severe consequences, as both Ananias and Sapphira fell dead after their lies were exposed.

The story of Ananias and Sapphira serves as a sobering reminder of the seriousness of sin, particularly in the context of the church. Their desire for recognition and approval led them to compromise their integrity and ultimately resulted in their demise. This narrative emphasizes the importance of honesty and transparency within the body of Christ.

Moreover, it reveals the gravity of lying to the Holy Spirit, highlighting how such actions can lead to spiritual death. The incident serves as a cautionary tale about the dangers of allowing pride and the desire for validation to guide our actions, reminding us to remain humble and truthful in our dealings with God and one another.

The Rich Young Ruler: The Cost of Disobedience

In Mark 10:17-22, we encounter the story of the rich young ruler who approaches Jesus seeking eternal life. Despite his adherence to the commandments, he is ultimately unwilling to part with his wealth when Jesus challenges him to sell all he has and give to the poor. The young ruler's refusal to follow Jesus highlights the danger of allowing material possessions to take precedence over spiritual commitment.

Jesus observes the young man's sorrow and states, "How hard it is for those who have riches to enter the kingdom of God!" (Mark 10:23). This encounter emphasizes that the acceptance of a Hell Bound Ticket can arise from a failure to prioritize God over worldly possessions. The rich young ruler's choice serves as a warning against the temptation to place material wealth above one's spiritual journey.

His story illustrates that it is not wealth itself that is the issue but the attachment to it. When individuals allow their possessions to dictate their choices, they risk accepting a ticket that leads away from God's purpose for their lives.

The Prodigal Son: The Journey to Destruction and Restoration

The parable of the Prodigal Son, found in Luke 15:11-32, beautifully encapsulates the themes of sin, rebellion, and the hope of redemption. In this story, the younger son demands his inheritance and leaves home to indulge in a life of reckless living. Initially, he enjoys the pleasures of sin but soon finds himself destitute and alone, far removed from his father's house.

This narrative illustrates the consequences of choosing a path of rebellion against God's design. The Prodigal Son's journey reflects how individuals can wander far from the truth, ultimately leading to despair and brokenness. However, the beauty of this parable lies in the son's eventual realization of his mistakes and his decision to return to his father.

When he returns, his father welcomes him with open arms, demonstrating the profound grace and mercy that God extends to those who repent. This story reminds us that even when we stray far from the path, there is always a way back to God. The Prodigal Son's experience points to the importance of recognizing our need for repentance and the transformative power of God's love.

Throughout these biblical narratives, we witness the common theme of sin and disobedience leading individuals down the wrong spiritual path. Each of these stories serves as a powerful reminder of the consequences of straying from God's will and the importance of remaining vigilant in our spiritual journeys.

The lives of Adam and Eve, Cain, Saul, David, Solomon, Judas Iscariot, Ananias and Sapphira, the rich young ruler, and the Prodigal Son all illustrate the perils of allowing sin to take root in our hearts. These narratives remind us of the need for repentance, accountability, and the continual pursuit of God's truth in our lives.

As we reflect on these examples, let us be vigilant in our walk with God, ensuring that we do not unknowingly accept a Hell Bound Ticket through our choices. The stories of these biblical figures urge us to seek God's guidance, remain steadfast in our faith, and embrace the grace and mercy that He offers to those who turn back to Him.

CHAPTER THREE

THE AMALEKITE SPIRIT AND THE SPIRITUAL ATTACK

Introduction to the Amalekite Spirit and Its Role in Weakening Believers

In our spiritual journey, we encounter various forces that seek to undermine our faith and lead us away from God's purpose. One of the most insidious of these forces is what we refer to as the Amalekite spirit. Rooted in the biblical account of the Amalekites, this spirit embodies traits of opposition, deception, and spiritual lethargy. Understanding the nature of the Amalekite spirit is crucial for every believer seeking to live a victorious life in Christ.

The Origin of the Amalekites

The Amalekites were a nomadic tribe descended from Esau, the brother of Jacob, and are first mentioned in the Book of Exodus. After the Israelites had escaped from slavery in Egypt, the Amalekites attacked them at Rephidim (Exodus 17:8-16). This attack was significant, as it marked one of the first military encounters faced by the Israelites as they journeyed toward the

Promised Land.

God viewed the Amalekites' attack as a direct challenge to His people and His plan. As a result, He declared war against them, instructing Moses to write down that He would completely blot out the memory of Amalek (Exodus 17:14). This declaration reveals the Amalekites' role as a symbol of spiritual opposition, serving as a constant reminder of the dangers that lurk in the shadows of our faith.

Characteristics of the Amalekite Spirit

The Amalekite spirit is characterized by several key traits that contribute to its effectiveness in undermining believers. Understanding these characteristics can help us recognize its presence in our lives and the lives of those around us.

Opposition to God's People: The Amalekites' primary role was to oppose the Israelites and thwart their progress toward the Promised Land. This spirit continues to manifest today by sowing discord, doubt, and fear among believers, seeking to derail them from their God-given destinies.

Deception and Manipulation: The Amalekite spirit thrives on deception, using lies and half-truths to lead believers astray. This manipulation can take many forms, including false teachings, misleading information, and the subtle temptation to compromise one's values.

Exploitation of Weakness: The Amalekites often attacked the weakest members of the Israelite community, targeting those who were lagging behind (Deuteronomy 25:17-18). This characteristic highlights the spirit's strategy of exploiting vulnerabilities, seeking to ensnare those who are spiritually weak or disconnected from the community of faith.

Complacency and Apathy: The Amalekite spirit promotes a sense of complacency among believers, encouraging a passive approach to faith. This spiritual lethargy can lead to a lack of vigilance, making it easier for the enemy to infiltrate and weaken the believer's resolve.

Bitterness and Division: The Amalekite spirit promotes bitterness and division within the body of Christ, creating rifts between believers and leading to a breakdown of community. By sowing seeds of discord, this spirit undermines unity and cooperation, which are essential for spiritual growth.

The Role of the Amalekite Spirit in Weakening Believers

The Amalekite spirit plays a significant role in weakening believers, hindering their spiritual growth, and ultimately leading them to accept a Hell Bound Ticket. This weakening occurs through various means, each designed to create doubt, confusion, and separation from God.

Spiritual Discouragement

One of the primary tactics of the Amalekite spirit is to discourage believers, instilling feelings of hopelessness and despair. This discouragement can manifest in several ways:

Failures and Setbacks: Believers may experience failures or setbacks in their personal lives, leading them to question their faith and God's faithfulness. The Amalekite spirit capitalizes on these moments of vulnerability, whispering lies that promote feelings of inadequacy and defeat.

Isolation: Discouragement often leads to isolation, as individuals withdraw from the faith community. The enemy knows that when believers are isolated, they become easier targets for spiritual attacks. They risk becoming disconnected from God's grace and encouragement by cutting themselves off from fellowship and support.

Loss of Vision: The Amalekite spirit seeks to diminish believers' vision for their lives, causing them to lose sight of God's promises. When individuals become discouraged, they may abandon their dreams and aspirations, accepting a state of complacency that ultimately leads to spiritual stagnation.

Temptation to Compromise

The Amalekite spirit also tempts believers to compromise their faith and values, leading them down a path of destruction. This compromise can take many forms:

Moral Laxity: The enemy often uses cultural pressures to encourage believers to lower their ethical standards. This can include engaging in behaviors contrary to biblical teachings, such as dishonesty, immorality, or unethical practices. When believers compromise their values, they risk accepting a Hell Bound Ticket that distances them from God's blessings.

Misplaced Priorities: The Amalekite spirit can lead believers to prioritize worldly concerns over their relationship with God. As individuals become consumed by pursuing success, wealth, or status, they may inadvertently neglect their spiritual lives, opening themselves up to the enemy's influence.

Peer Pressure: The desire for acceptance and approval can cause believers to compromise their convictions in the face of peer pressure. The Amalekite spirit exploits these desires, encouraging individuals to conform to societal norms rather than standing firm in their faith.

Spiritual Distraction

Distraction is another powerful weapon wielded by the Amalekite spirit. The enemy seeks to weaken their resolve and hinder their spiritual growth by diverting believers' attention from God and His word. This distraction can occur in various ways:

Busy Schedules: In today's fast-paced world, many believers are overwhelmed with responsibilities, commitments, and distractions. The Amalekite spirit thrives in these moments, causing individuals to neglect their spiritual disciplines, such as prayer and Bible study.

Social Media and Entertainment: The pervasive influence of social media and entertainment can lead to spiritual distraction, pulling believers away from their focus on God. The enemy uses these platforms to fill hearts and minds with noise, drowning out the still, small voice of the Holy Spirit.

Unproductive Relationships: Engaging in relationships that do not contribute to spiritual growth can lead to distraction. The Amalekite spirit can use these relationships to divert believers from their purpose, keeping them focused on the mundane rather than the divine.

Encouraging Bitterness and Resentment

The Amalekite spirit thrives on bitterness and resentment, using these emotions to create division and discord within the body of Christ. When believers harbor unforgiveness or resentment, they risk becoming vessels for the enemy's agenda:

Resentment Toward Others: Bitterness can easily take root when individuals feel wronged or hurt by others. The Amalekite spirit exploits these feelings, encouraging individuals to dwell on past grievances rather than seeking reconciliation.

Division in the Church: When bitterness festers, it can lead to division. The enemy uses this division to weaken the body of Christ, hindering its effectiveness in fulfilling God's mission.

Inability to Move Forward: Holding onto bitterness can prevent individuals from experiencing God's healing and restoration. The Amalekite spirit seeks to keep believers trapped in a cycle of unforgiveness, ultimately leading to spiritual stagnation.

Spiritual Complacency

Finally, the Amalekite spirit promotes complacency among believers, encouraging a passive approach to faith. This spiritual lethargy can have detrimental effects:

Loss of Passion: When believers become complacent, they may lose their passion for God and His work. The fire that once burned brightly in their hearts may fade, leaving them vulnerable to spiritual attacks.

Lack of Accountability: Complacency can lead to a lack of accountability, making it easier for individuals to drift away from their faith. When believers no longer engage in meaningful relationships with others, they become susceptible to the enemy's influence.

Failure to Grow: Spiritual complacency stunts growth, preventing individuals from experiencing the fullness of God's promises. When believers fail to pursue their faith actively, they risk becoming stagnant, allowing the Amalekite spirit to gain a foothold.

Recognizing the Amalekite Spirit in Our Lives

To combat the Amalekite spirit effectively, believers must first recognize its presence. This requires self-examination and discernment, allowing the Holy Spirit to reveal areas of weakness or compromise. Here are some practical steps for recognizing the Amalekite spirit:

Evaluate Your Spiritual Health: Regularly assess your spiritual well-being through prayer and reflection. Are you growing in your relationship with God, or have you become complacent? Are you actively seeking to live in obedience to His Word?

Identify Areas of Distraction: Take note of the distractions in your life that may be pulling you away from God. Consider whether social media, entertainment, or unproductive relationships hinder your spiritual growth.

Examine Your Relationships: Evaluate the influence of those around you. Are your relationships encouraging you in your faith, or are they leading you toward compromise? Surround yourself with individuals who inspire and challenge you to grow in your walk with God.

Seek Accountability: Find a trusted friend or mentor to hold you accountable in your spiritual journey. Regular check-ins and honest discussions can help you remain vigilant against the influence of the Amalekite spirit.

Embrace a Spirit of Forgiveness: Work on letting go of bitterness and resentment, allowing God's grace to flow through you. This may involve confronting past hurts and forgiving those who have wronged you.

Pursue Spiritual Disciplines: Engage in spiritual practices such as prayer, Bible study, and worship to strengthen your relationship with God. These disciplines can help you remain focused on His promises and protect you from complacency.

Overcoming the Amalekite Spirit

While the Amalekite spirit poses a significant threat to believers, the good news is that we can overcome it through Christ. By relying on the Holy Spirit and actively pursuing a life of obedience, we can effectively combat the influence of this spirit. Here are some strategies for overcoming the Amalekite spirit:

Embrace Your Identity in Christ: Understand that you are a child of God, redeemed and empowered by His Spirit. Recognizing your identity in Christ equips you to stand firm against the enemy's lies and deception.

Engage in Spiritual Warfare: Use the authority given to you as a believer to confront the Amalekite spirit. Ephesians 6:12 reminds us that our struggle is not against flesh and blood but against spiritual forces. Arm yourself with the whole armor of God, including prayer, the Word, and faith, to resist the enemy.

Join a Community of Faith: Surround yourself with fellow believers who encourage and uplift you. The power of community

THE MYSTERY OF THE HELL BOUND TICKET

cannot be underestimated in our spiritual battles. Together, you can support one another, pray for each other, and hold one another accountable.

Embrace a Heart of Worship: Engage in worship as a means of drawing closer to God. Worship shifts our focus from our problems and distractions to the greatness of our God. It serves as a powerful weapon against the enemy's attacks.

Prioritize Prayer and Scripture: Develop a consistent prayer life and immerse yourself in the Word of God. These practices strengthen your faith, deepen your relationship with God, and equip you to resist the Amalekite spirit.

Practice Forgiveness: Let go of bitterness and resentment by choosing to forgive those who have wronged you. This act of obedience opens the door to healing and restoration, freeing you from the grip of the Amalekite spirit.

The Amalekite spirit poses a significant threat to believers, seeking to undermine their faith and weaken their resolve. By understanding its characteristics and recognizing its influence in our lives, we can take proactive steps to combat its effects. Through self-examination, accountability, and reliance on God's power, we can overcome the Amalekite spirit and walk in the victory that Christ has secured for us.

How Satan Targets People in Their Weakest Moments

In the spiritual battle that every believer faces, understanding how the enemy operates is important. One of the primary tactics employed by Satan is to target individuals in their weakest moments. These moments of vulnerability can arise from various sources, stress, loss, disappointment, or spiritual dryness. The enemy is acutely aware of our weaknesses and seeks to exploit them, leading us further away from God's purpose.

Spiritual weakness can manifest in various ways, often characterized by a lack of faith, feelings of inadequacy, or emotional distress. It is essential to recognize the signs of spiritual weakness to understand how the enemy may attempt to exploit these vulnerabilities.

Emotional Turmoil: Emotional struggles, such as anxiety, depression, and grief, can significantly impact a believer's spiritual health. When individuals are consumed by negative emotions, they may find it challenging to connect with God, making them susceptible to the enemy's lies.

Physical Exhaustion: Physical well-being is essential to spiritual health. Our ability to resist temptation diminishes when we are physically drained due to lack of sleep, poor nutrition, or overwhelming stress. The enemy often capitalizes on physical exhaustion, making it easier for us to give in to sin.

Isolation: During moments of weakness, individuals may withdraw from their community of faith, feeling ashamed or defeated. This isolation can create an environment where the enemy can attack without opposition. When alone, we are more vulnerable to the enemy's deceptions and can become trapped in negative thought patterns.

Spiritual Apathy: Spiritual dryness and apathy can lead to a lack of motivation to pursue God. When believers become complacent in their faith, they may neglect spiritual disciplines such as prayer and Bible study, leaving them vulnerable to the enemy's influence.

Doubt and Uncertainty: Doubt is a powerful weapon the enemy uses to sow seeds of confusion and fear. During challenging times, believers may question their faith, God's goodness, or His promises. This doubt can create a breeding ground for spiritual attacks.

Strategies Employed by Satan

Recognizing how Satan targets believers in their weakest moments requires an understanding of his strategies. The enemy employs various tactics to exploit our vulnerabilities, leading us away from God and His truth.

Temptation: One of the enemy's primary strategies is temptation. When believers struggle emotionally or spiritually, they may be more susceptible to sinful behaviors. Satan may present enticing alternatives that promise immediate gratification, distracting individuals from their commitment to God.

An individual facing emotional turmoil may seek comfort in unhealthy habits such as substance abuse or inappropriate relationships. The enemy exploits their pain, offering false solutions that lead to further spiritual bondage.

Accusation: The enemy is known as the "accuser of the brethren" (Revelation 12:10). In moments of weakness, he seeks to remind believers of their past failures, sowing doubt and shame. These accusations can lead to feelings of unworthiness and distance from God.

A believer who has struggled with sin may experience guilt and shame when they falter again. The enemy capitalizes on these feelings, convincing them that they are beyond redemption and unworthy of God's love.

Distraction: Satan uses distraction to divert believers' attention from God's truth. During moments of vulnerability, individuals may find themselves consumed by worldly concerns, entertainment, or social media, which can lead to a diminished focus on spiritual matters.

People experiencing spiritual dryness may binge-watch television shows or scroll through social media instead of praying or worship. This distraction keeps them from experiencing God's presence and guidance.

Deception: The enemy is a master deceiver, often twisting God's Word or presenting false teachings to lead believers astray. Individuals may be more prone to accept deceptive ideas that contradict biblical truths during moments of doubt or confusion.

A believer struggling with unanswered prayers may encounter false teachings that suggest their faith is insufficient or that God does not care about their needs. These deceptions can further erode their faith.

Fear: Fear is a powerful weapon that Satan uses to paralyze believers and prevent them from taking action. When individuals are in a state of weakness, fear can manifest in various ways, including fear of failure, rejection, or the unknown.

A believer who feels called to a particular ministry may experience fear about stepping out in faith. The enemy exploits this fear, leading them to doubt their abilities and withdraw from God's calling.

Biblical Examples of Spiritual Weakness and Attack

Throughout the Bible, we find examples of individuals who faced significant challenges during their weakest moments, illustrating how Satan targeted them. These accounts serve as powerful reminders of the need for vigilance and reliance on God during times of weakness.

Job: The Test of Faith: Job, a righteous man, suffered immensely when he lost his wealth, health, and family. In his weakest moments, Satan sought to undermine his faith by instigating doubt about God's goodness and justice. Job's friends, who initially came to comfort him, ultimately added to his pain by questioning his integrity. Despite his struggles, Job remained steadfast in his faith, demonstrating the importance of perseverance and trust in God during adversity (Job 1-2).

Peter: The Danger of Spiritual Overconfidence: Apostle Peter, known for his boldness, experienced a moment of weakness when he denied Jesus three times during His trial. Despite his earlier declaration that he would never forsake Jesus (Matthew 26:33), Peter succumbed to fear and pressure in his weakest moment. This incident underscores the importance of humility and the need for vigilance against the enemy's attacks, even for those who are strong in faith.

Elijah: The Weight of Discouragement: After a triumphant victory over the prophets of Baal, the prophet Elijah fled from Queen Jezebel, who sought to take his life. In his moment of discouragement and fear, Elijah isolated himself and fell into despair, asking God to take his life (1 Kings 19:4). Satan used Elijah's vulnerability to plant seeds of doubt about his purpose and value. However, God ministered to Elijah, reminding him that he was not alone and had a greater purpose.

David: The Consequences of Complacency: King David, a man after God's own heart, experienced a moment of spiritual weakness when he neglected his duties and fell into sin with Bathsheba. While he was supposed to be at war, he remained in the palace, leading to complacency and moral failure (2 Samuel 11). David's story serves as a reminder that even the strongest believers can fall into sin if they allow complacency to take root in their lives.

Judas Iscariot: The Betrayal Driven by Greed: Judas, one of Jesus' closest disciples, succumbed to greed during a moment of weakness. After witnessing Jesus' miracles and teachings, he betrayed the Son of God for thirty pieces of silver (Matthew 26:14-16). Judas's choice to prioritize material gain over his relationship with Jesus illustrates how vulnerability to temptation can lead to devastating consequences.

Fortifying Ourselves Against Attacks

Recognizing how Satan targets us in our weakest moments is the first step toward fortification against his attacks. Below are practical steps believers can take to strengthen themselves against the enemy's schemes:

Build a Strong Foundation in Prayer: Consistent prayer is essential for spiritual resilience. Engaging in daily communication with

God helps fortify our faith and provides the strength to withstand attacks. In Philippians 4:6-7, we are reminded to present our requests to God through prayer, which will guard our hearts and minds.

Engage with Scripture: The word of God serves as our primary weapon against the enemy. By immersing ourselves in Scripture, we can equip ourselves with the truth to counter deception. Jesus demonstrated this during His temptation in the wilderness, using Scripture to refute Satan's lies (Matthew 4:1-11).

Seek Community Support: Surrounding ourselves with fellow believers provides encouragement, accountability, and support during difficult times. Engaging in a community of faith allows us to share our struggles and receive prayer and guidance, which can help us stay grounded in our faith.

Recognize and Acknowledge Weakness: Understanding our weaknesses is crucial for spiritual growth. We can develop strategies to combat temptation and vulnerability by acknowledging areas where we struggle. This self-awareness allows us to seek God's help and strength proactively.

Develop Healthy Coping Mechanisms: We should develop healthy coping mechanisms instead of turning to unhealthy habits or distractions during moments of weakness. This may include engaging in physical activity, practicing mindfulness, or pursuing hobbies that uplift our spirits and draw us closer to God.

Practice Self-Examination: Regularly assessing our spiritual health helps us identify potential vulnerabilities. This self-examination allows us to address issues before they escalate, ensuring we remain steadfast in our faith.

Embrace a Heart of Worship: Worship shifts our focus from our problems to God's greatness. Whether through music, prayer, or other forms of expression, engaging in worship helps us cultivate a heart that seeks God above all else.

Rely on the Holy Spirit: The Holy Spirit is our Comforter and Helper, guiding us in moments of weakness. Leaning on the Holy Spirit for strength and wisdom empowers us to resist temptation and remain anchored in our faith.

Satan's strategy of targeting believers in their weakest moments reminds us of the importance of vigilance and dependence on God. By understanding how the enemy exploits our vulnerabilities, we can take proactive steps to fortify ourselves against his attacks. Through prayer, Scripture engagement, community support, and reliance on the Holy Spirit, we can navigate the challenges of our faith with strength and resilience.

CHAPTER FOUR

SPIRITUAL DECEPTION AND DISTRACTION

How The Enemy Uses Deception
to Keep People Bound

I n the journey of faith, one of the most insidious tactics employed by the enemy is deception. Satan, described as "the father of lies" (John 8:44), utilizes deceit to keep believers bound in spiritual chains, preventing them from experiencing the fullness of God's promises. Understanding the nature of spiritual deception and the distractions it creates is crucial for every believer seeking to walk in truth and freedom.

The Nature of Spiritual Deception

Sspiritual deception can be defined as a distortion of truth that leads individuals away from God and His word. It often masquerades as wisdom, insight, or enlightenment, drawing people in with appealing promises that ultimately lead to spiritual bondage. The enemy's tactics are subtle and cunning, designed to exploit the weaknesses and desires of the human heart.

Misinterpretation of Scripture: One of the enemy's primary methods of deception is the misinterpretation of Scripture. Satan often twists God's word, taking verses out of context or applying them in ways that align with his agenda. For instance, during Jesus' temptation in the wilderness, Satan quoted Psalm 91:11-12 to entice Jesus into throwing Himself off the temple, misapplying God's promise of protection (Matthew 4:5-7). This illustrates how the enemy can distort Scripture to lead believers astray.

False Teachings: The proliferation of false teachings is another significant aspect of spiritual deception. In recent years, the rise of the prosperity gospel, universalism, and other misleading doctrines has created confusion among believers. These teachings often prioritize personal gain or acceptance over obedience to God's Word, distorting the true nature of the Gospel.

Cultural Influence: Our culture can also be a source of spiritual deception. Many societal norms and values run counter to biblical principles. As believers, we must be vigilant against subtle messages that promote compromise or challenge our faith. The enemy exploits cultural pressures to draw believers away from God's truth.

Self-Deception: Perhaps one of the most dangerous forms of deception is self-deception. This occurs when individuals convince themselves they are in the right standing with God while living in disobedience. This can manifest as rationalizing sinful behavior, believing that God's grace excuses persistent wrongdoing, or disregarding the conviction of the Holy Spirit.

The Tactics of Deception

Satan employs various tactics to ensure that deception takes root in believers' hearts and minds. Understanding these tactics is essential for identifying and resisting the enemy's influence.

Lies About Identity: One of the most effective ways the enemy deceives individuals is by distorting their understanding of their identity in Christ. When believers doubt their worth or identity as children of God, they become vulnerable to deception. The enemy whispers lies, undermining their confidence and leading them to seek validation in worldly pursuits.

A believer may feel inadequate and believe they are not good enough for God's love or purpose. This lie can lead them to seek fulfillment in unhealthy relationships or material possessions, ultimately trapping them in spiritual bondage.

Encouraging Doubt: Doubt is a powerful tool in the enemy's arsenal. By planting seeds of uncertainty regarding God's character, promises, and faithfulness, Satan seeks to create a barrier between believers and their faith. Doubt can arise in various forms, such as questioning God's goodness in times of suffering or doubting the effectiveness of prayer.

When believers experience a personal tragedy, they may question God's love and purpose. This doubt can lead them to withdraw from their faith community, further isolating them and allowing deception to take hold.

Distraction from Spiritual Disciplines: The enemy knows that when believers neglect spiritual disciplines such as prayer, Bible study, and worship, they become more susceptible to deception. By introducing distractions, whether through busyness, entertainment, or societal pressures, the enemy seeks to divert attention away from God's truth.

A believer may find themselves overwhelmed with work or family commitments, leading them to prioritize these responsibilities over their relationship with God. This distraction can create a spiritual vacuum, making them more vulnerable to deception.

Promising Immediate Gratification: The enemy often presents sinful behavior as a solution to life's challenges, promising immediate gratification and relief from pain. By appealing to human desires, Satan entices individuals to compromise their faith and engage in behaviors that lead to spiritual bondage.

A person facing emotional distress may turn to substance abuse or unhealthy coping mechanisms, believing that these actions will provide temporary relief. However, such choices ultimately lead to deeper spiritual and emotional issues.

Creating a Sense of False Security: The enemy may lead believers to believe they are secure in their faith, even when living in disobedience. This false sense of security can prevent individuals from recognizing their need for repentance and growth, allowing deception to flourish.

A believer may attend church regularly, serve in ministry, and engage in outwardly righteous behaviors while harboring unconfessed sin. The enemy uses this façade to keep them bound in deception, preventing them from experiencing true freedom in Christ.

The Consequences of Spiritual Deception

The consequences of spiritual deception are profound and far-reaching. When individuals fall victim to the enemy's lies, they risk entering a cycle of disobedience that leads to spiritual bondage.

Loss of Joy and Peace: Deception creates a barrier between believers and the joy and peace of a genuine relationship with God. When individuals live in disobedience or embrace lies, they often experience a lack of fulfillment and inner turmoil.

A believer who is engaging in a sinful relationship may initially feel pleasure but will eventually experience guilt and shame, leading to emotional distress and spiritual emptiness.

Separation from God: Spiritual deception can lead to a breakdown in the relationship between believers and God. When individuals believe the enemy's lies, they may withdraw from God's presence, creating a spiritual distance that hinders their growth and understanding of His truth.

A person who feels unworthy due to past mistakes may avoid prayer and fellowship, believing that they have disqualified themselves from God's love. This separation reinforces the enemy's deception and deepens their sense of isolation.

Inability to Discern Truth: Spiritual deception clouds one's ability to discern truth from falsehood. When individuals become accustomed to living in deception, they may struggle to recognize God's voice and guidance, leaving them vulnerable to further lies.

A believer may accept false teachings or compromise their values due to a lack of discernment, leading them further away from God's truth.

Destruction of Relationships: Deception can also lead to the breakdown of relationships with others. When lies ensnare individuals, they may struggle with trust, resentment, and bitterness, creating division within their relationships.

A believer who harbors unforgiveness due to deception may alienate friends and family, causing pain and conflict that further perpetuates their bondage.

Recognizing and Combating Deception

To effectively combat spiritual deception, believers must develop a discerning spirit and actively engage in practices that promote spiritual growth. Below are some practical steps to help recognize and resist the enemy's deception:

Ground Yourself in Scripture: Familiarizing oneself with the word of God is crucial for discernment. By studying Scripture, believers can equip themselves with the truth to counter the enemy's lies. Regularly reading and meditating on God's Word helps establish a firm faith foundation.

Consider setting aside dedicated time each day for Bible study. Use devotionals or study guides to deepen your understanding of Scripture and apply its truths to your life.

Have a Prayer Life: Consistent prayer is essential for spiritual vigilance. Through worship, believers can seek God's guidance, strength, and wisdom in navigating their challenges. Prayer also aligns one's heart and mind with God's truth.

Establish a prayer routine that includes both spoken and silent prayer. Seek God's guidance in areas where you may be susceptible to deception.

Seek Accountability and Fellowship: Surrounding oneself with a community of believers provides support, encouragement, and accountability. Engaging in fellowship allows individuals to share struggles, pray for one another, and grow together in faith.

Join a small group or Bible study to build relationships with fellow believers. Openly share your struggles and seek accountability in your spiritual journey.

Practice Discernment: Developing discernment involves evaluating teachings, beliefs, and influences in light of Scripture. Believers must learn to recognize the voice of the Holy Spirit and seek God's wisdom in making decisions.

Before accepting new teachings or ideas, take time to pray and study Scripture to determine their alignment with God's Word. Seek guidance from trusted spiritual mentors.

Engage in Spiritual Warfare: Recognizing that the battle against deception is spiritual in nature is vital. Believers are called to engage in spiritual warfare through prayer, declaring God's truth, and standing firm against the enemy's schemes.

Arm yourself with the full armor of God as described in Ephesians 6:10-18. Pray for strength and wisdom to resist the enemy's attacks and stand firm in your faith.

Embrace Truth and Reject Lies: Actively reject the lies that the enemy seeks to implant in your mind and heart. Affirm your identity in Christ and embrace the truth of His Word.

Create a list of Scriptures that affirm your identity and worth in Christ. Use these verses as declarations to counter the lies you may encounter.

Practice Forgiveness: Letting go of bitterness and resentment is essential for spiritual freedom. Choose to forgive those who have wronged you, allowing God's grace to flow through you.

Reflect on any unresolved bitterness in your heart. Pray for the strength to forgive and seek reconciliation where possible.

Spiritual deception is a powerful weapon wielded by the enemy to keep believers bound and hinder their relationship with God. By understanding the nature of deception, recognizing its tactics, and actively engaging in practices that promote spiritual growth, believers can fortify themselves against the enemy's schemes.

The Consequences of Distraction in Spiritual Warfare

In the spiritual journey of every believer, distraction can prove to be one of the most formidable obstacles to faith. The enemy skillfully uses distractions to divert attention away from God, His Word, and the purpose He has for our lives. When believers become preoccupied with worldly concerns, entertainment, or even legitimate responsibilities, they can easily lose sight of their spiritual goals.

The Nature of Distraction

Distraction can be defined as anything that diverts our attention from our primary focus or purpose. In the context of spiritual warfare, distraction can manifest in various forms, including:

Worldly Concerns: Everyday responsibilities such as work, family, and social obligations can become overwhelming, leading individuals to prioritize these concerns over their relationship with God.

Entertainment and Media: The pervasive influence of media, including television, social media, and the internet, can create a constant barrage of distractions that pull believers away from spiritual pursuits.

Fear and Anxiety: Emotional struggles such as fear and anxiety can divert our focus from God's promises and lead us to dwell on negative thoughts and situations.

Personal Ambitions: While ambition can be a positive force, it can also lead to distractions when individuals become more focused on their goals and achievements than on their relationship with God.

Relational Conflicts: Interpersonal issues and conflicts can create emotional turmoil that draws believers' attention away from their spiritual walk, making it challenging to remain focused on God.

Consequences of Distraction

Distraction in spiritual warfare can lead to several detrimental consequences that hinder a believer's spiritual growth and effectiveness. Below are some key consequences that arise from distraction:

Spiritual Stagnation

Distraction often results in spiritual stagnation, where believers find themselves in a state of complacency rather than growth. When individuals become preoccupied with worldly concerns or entertainment, they may neglect spiritual disciplines such as prayer, Bible study, and worship.

A believer who once fervently pursued God may find themselves drifting away from their faith due to distractions from work or social media. Without consistent engagement in spiritual practices, their relationship with God begins to suffer, leading to a lack of spiritual vitality.

The consequence of spiritual stagnation is profound, as it can create a cycle of complacency that becomes increasingly difficult to break. The longer individuals remain distracted, the less likely they are to recognize their need for spiritual growth or change.

Vulnerability to Deception

Distraction creates an environment where believers become more susceptible to deception. When individuals are not grounded in God's word and focused on their relationship with Him, they may be easily swayed by false teachings or misleading ideas.

A believer who spends minimal time in Scripture and prayer may encounter teachings that contradict biblical truths without the discernment needed to recognize the deception. This can lead to confusion about their faith and values, making them more vulnerable to the enemy's lies.

The increased susceptibility to deception can create a domino effect, leading to a further decline in spiritual health. As individuals become more influenced by falsehoods, their ability to discern truth diminishes, resulting in a distorted understanding of God's character and promises.

Disruption of Relationships

Distractions can also lead to the disruption of relationships within the body of Christ. When individuals prioritize distractions over meaningful connections, they risk alienating themselves from fellow believers and missing out on the support and encouragement that comes from community.

A believer who becomes consumed by their job may neglect their relationships with friends or family, leading to feelings of isolation. This isolation can create emotional distance, making it difficult to engage in spiritual fellowship or accountability.

The disruption of relationships can have significant consequences for spiritual growth. God designed the body of Christ to work together in unity, and when distractions hinder connection, believers may struggle to receive the encouragement and support they need to persevere in their faith.

Loss of Focus on God's Purpose

Distraction can lead to a loss of focus on God's purpose for our lives. When believers become sidetracked by the demands of daily life or the allure of worldly pursuits, they may forget the calling and mission God has placed on their hearts.

A person who feels called to serve in ministry may become distracted by career aspirations, leading them to forgo their calling. This loss of focus can create feelings of unfulfillment and frustration, as individuals find themselves living outside of God's design.

When believers lose sight of their purpose, they may miss opportunities to fulfill God's plans for their lives. Distraction can prevent them from stepping into their God-given assignments, leading to a sense of spiritual disconnection.

Increased Fear and Anxiety

Distraction often breeds fear and anxiety, as individuals become overwhelmed by the pressures of life. When believers allow distractions to dominate their focus, they may struggle to trust in God's sovereignty and provision.

A believer facing financial difficulties may become consumed by worry and anxiety, leading them to seek solutions apart from God. This fear can prevent them from experiencing the peace that comes from relying on God's promises.

The cycle of distraction, fear, and anxiety can be debilitating, preventing individuals from experiencing the freedom and joy that comes from a vibrant relationship with God. This emotional turmoil can further hinder spiritual growth, creating a barrier between believers and the fullness of God's presence.

Compromised Integrity

Distraction can also lead to compromised integrity as individuals become entangled in sinful behaviors or questionable choices. When believers allow distractions to take precedence over their commitment to God, they may find themselves making decisions that do not align with their faith.

A believer may justify unethical behavior at work due to pressure or distraction, leading them to compromise their values. This compromise can create a cycle of guilt and shame that further distances them from God.

The consequences of compromised integrity can have lasting effects, as they can damage one's witness and testimony. When individuals engage in behaviors contrary to their faith, they risk losing credibility in the eyes of others, hindering their ability to share the Gospel effectively.

Diminished Spiritual Authority

Distraction can also diminish a believer's spiritual authority. When individuals are not actively engaging in their relationship with God, they may find it challenging to exercise the authority that comes from their identity in Christ.

A believer who neglects prayer and spiritual disciplines may find themselves ill-equipped to confront spiritual battles or to minister to others effectively. This diminishment of authority can lead to a sense of inadequacy and fear, preventing them from stepping into their God-given calling.

A diminished sense of spiritual authority can create a cycle of self-doubt and fear, further entrenching believers in distraction and disobedience. Without recognizing their authority in Christ, individuals may become passive in their faith, allowing the enemy to operate unchallenged.

Strategies to Combat Distraction

To overcome the consequences of distraction, believers must be proactive in establishing practices that help them maintain focus on God and His purpose. Here are practical strategies for combating distraction in spiritual warfare:

Establish Priorities: Identify what truly matters in your spiritual journey and establish priorities accordingly. Consider allocating specific time for prayer, Bible study, and fellowship to ensure that your spiritual life remains central.

Create a daily or weekly schedule that includes dedicated time for spiritual disciplines. Treat this time as an essential appointment, prioritizing it above other activities.

Limit Media Consumption: Be mindful of the media you consume and the impact it has on your spiritual life. Reducing screen time and limiting exposure to distracting content can create space for spiritual growth.

Set boundaries for your media consumption, including social media and entertainment. Consider designating specific times for media use to avoid mindless scrolling or binge-watching.

Practice Mindfulness: Engage in mindfulness practices that help you stay present and focused on God. Mindfulness allows you to recognize distractions and redirect your attention toward God's truth.

Incorporate mindfulness techniques, such as deep breathing, prayer, or meditation, into your daily routine. Use these moments to refocus your thoughts on God and His promises.

Engage in Fellowship: Surround yourself with a community of believers who encourage and challenge you to grow in your faith. Engaging in fellowship helps combat isolation and provides accountability.

Join a small group or Bible study where you can connect with others in meaningful ways. Share your struggles and encourage one another to stay focused on spiritual pursuits.

Seek God's Guidance: Regularly seek God's guidance and wisdom in your life. By praying for discernment and clarity, you can navigate distractions and remain anchored in God's truth.

Set aside time for intentional prayer, asking God to reveal areas where you may be distracted or compromised. Listen for His guidance and respond with obedience.

Cultivate Gratitude: Developing an attitude of gratitude can help shift your focus away from distractions and toward God's blessings. When you recognize and appreciate God's goodness in your life, it becomes easier to remain anchored in faith.

Keep a gratitude journal, noting things you are thankful for each day. Reflecting on God's blessings can help combat feelings of distraction and discontentment.

Engage in Service: Serving others can help combat distraction and refocus your attention on God's purpose. When you actively engage in acts of service, you remind yourself of the calling to love and serve those around you.

Look for opportunities to serve in your church or community. Engaging in service can help you maintain a sense of purpose and connection to God's mission.

Distraction is a powerful weapon employed by the enemy in spiritual warfare. By understanding the nature and consequences of distraction, believers can take proactive steps to combat its influence in their lives. Through prioritizing spiritual disciplines, establishing healthy boundaries, engaging in fellowship, and seeking God's guidance, individuals can remain focused on their relationship with God and His purpose.

CHAPTER FIVE

CANCELING THE HELLBOUND TICKET

*Steps to Spiritually Reject and
Cancel the Hellbound Ticket*

T he journey of faith is a continual process of choosing life over death, truth over deception, and righteousness over sin. While the enemy offers a Hellbound ticket to those who fall prey to his lies and temptations, the power of God through Christ enables us to cancel and reject this ticket. Regardless of past choices or the strength of the enemy's influence, believers have the authority to reclaim their spiritual standing and secure their future in God's Kingdom.

Before diving into the steps of canceling the Hellbound ticket, it is important to understand why such a cancellation is necessary. The Hellbound ticket represents spiritual death, separation from God, and alignment with the enemy's agenda. It is not always accepted knowingly; often, individuals find themselves spiritually compromised through subtle compromises, habitual sin, or disobedience.

A believer who once walked in faith may find themselves entangled in sinful habits or worldly distractions, unaware of the extent to which they have accepted a Hellbound ticket. Over time, they may feel distanced from God, their prayers becoming less fervent, and their desire for spiritual growth waning.

The good news is that God, in His infinite grace and mercy, has provided a way out. The sacrifice of Jesus Christ on the cross is the ultimate cancellation of the Hellbound ticket. Through His blood, believers are redeemed, forgiven, and given the opportunity to repent, renounce sin, and walk in newness of life. But to fully experience this redemption, believers must actively engage in the process of rejecting and canceling the ticket that leads to spiritual destruction.

Step 1: Acknowledge the Need for Repentance

The first and most critical step in canceling the Hellbound ticket is acknowledgment. Recognizing the need for repentance is essential to begin the process of spiritual renewal. Many people may deny or minimize their sins, excusing them as minor errors or lapses in judgment. However, without honest acknowledgment of wrongdoing, it is impossible to experience the full forgiveness and restoration that God offers.

1 John 1:9 reminds us, "If we confess our sins, He is faithful and just to forgive us our sins and to cleanse us from all unrighteousness." Confession requires humility and transparency, both with God and ourselves. It involves taking full responsibility for actions, thoughts, and behaviors that are contrary to God's Word.

A believer who struggles with lying may initially justify their dishonesty by claiming that it protects others from harm or spares feelings. However, true repentance requires acknowledging that dishonesty is a sin, no matter the justification, and confessing this before God.

Acknowledgment leads to the awareness that we cannot cancel the Hellbound ticket on our own. It is only through God's intervention and the power of repentance that we can turn away from the spiritual path of destruction.

Step 2: Engage in Genuine Repentance

Repentance is more than a mere apology for wrongdoing; it is a heartfelt turning away from sin and a commitment to live in accordance with God's commands. In the process of canceling the Hellbound ticket, repentance plays a foundational role because it involves a complete change of direction—both spiritually and behaviorally.

Acts 3:19 calls believers to "Repent therefore and be converted, that your sins may be blotted out, so that times of refreshing may come from the presence of the Lord." This verse emphasizes the connection between repentance and spiritual renewal. It is through repentance that the Hellbound ticket is effectively canceled, and believers are restored to a state of grace.

True repentance consists of several key elements:
Sorrow for Sin: This involves feeling genuine remorse for the actions, behaviors, or attitudes that have separated us from God. It is important to note that this sorrow is not merely regret over the consequences of sin but a deep understanding of how sin grieves the heart of God.

A believer who has engaged in gossip may feel guilty about hurting someone's reputation, but genuine repentance goes beyond guilt, it is the recognition that such behavior displeases God and violates His standard of love and unity.

Turning Away from Sin: Repentance requires a decisive break from sinful behaviors and habits. It is not enough to feel remorse without making changes in one's lifestyle. A believer who seeks to cancel the Hellbound ticket must be willing to sever ties with anything that leads them away from God.

If a believer struggles with addiction, true repentance means taking practical steps to break free from that addiction, whether through seeking counseling, accountability, or avoiding environments that trigger temptation.

Commitment to Obedience: The ultimate goal of repentance is to align our lives with God's will. This means pursuing obedience in every area of life, allowing the Holy Spirit to guide us toward righteousness. Repentance is not a one-time act but a continual commitment to walking in God's ways.

A believer who repents from dishonesty must commit to living a life of truthfulness, even when it is difficult or inconvenient. This ongoing obedience is evidence that repentance is genuine.

Step 3: Renounce the Enemy's Lies and Deceptions

After repentance, the next critical step in canceling the Hellbound ticket is renunciation. The enemy operates through lies and deception, convincing individuals that they are unworthy of God's forgiveness or that their sin is too great to be overcome. To cancel the Hellbound ticket, believers must actively reject and renounce the lies that the enemy has used to keep them bound.

John 8:44 describes Satan as "the father of lies," and it is through these lies that he seeks to distort our perception of God and ourselves. Renouncing the enemy's lies means confronting these falsehoods with the truth of God's word.

Renouncing Lies About Identity: One of the most common lies that the enemy uses is to convince believers that they are unworthy of God's love and forgiveness. These lies may manifest as feelings of shame, guilt, or inadequacy.

A believer who has committed serious sins may believe that they are beyond redemption, hearing the enemy's voice whisper, "You are unworthy. God cannot forgive someone like you." To cancel the Hellbound ticket, the believer must renounce this lie and replace it with the truth found in Romans 8:1: "There is therefore now no condemnation to those who are in Christ Jesus."

Renouncing Lies About Sin: The enemy also seeks to minimize the seriousness of sin, encouraging believers to rationalize or justify their behaviors. Renouncing these lies means acknowledging that sin, no matter how small, is an offense to God and must be addressed.

A believer who struggles with dishonesty may hear the enemy's voice saying, "It's just a small lie, it doesn't really matter." Renouncing this lie means recognizing that even small sins have significant spiritual consequences and must be brought to God in repentance.

Renouncing Lies About God's Nature: The enemy often distorts our understanding of God's character, leading us to believe that God is distant, unloving, or unwilling to forgive. Renouncing these lies involves embracing the truth of God's love, grace, and willingness to restore.

A believer facing difficulties may be tempted to believe that God has abandoned them or no longer cares about their struggles. To cancel the Hellbound ticket, they must renounce this lie and declare the truth found in Psalm 34:18: "The Lord is near to those who have a broken heart, and saves such as have a contrite spirit."

Renunciation is not a passive process but an active confrontation of the enemy's tactics. Through prayer, declaration of God's truth, and reliance on the Holy Spirit, believers can break free from the lies that have kept them bound and cancel the Hellbound ticket once and for all.

Step 4: Embrace Forgiveness and Freedom in Christ

One of the most beautiful aspects of canceling the Hellbound ticket is experiencing the forgiveness and freedom that Christ offers. When believers repent, renounce the enemy's lies, and turn back to God, they are met with grace, mercy, and unconditional love. Forgiveness is not something that must be earned; it is a gift freely given to all who seek it.

1 John 1:7 states, "But if we walk in the light as He is in the light,

we have fellowship with one another, and the blood of Jesus Christ His Son cleanses us from all sin." This cleansing is a complete and total act of forgiveness, removing the stain of sin and restoring believers to their rightful place in God's family.

Receiving God's Forgiveness: Accepting forgiveness means recognizing that God's grace is sufficient to cover all sin, no matter how great. It also means releasing the guilt and shame associated with past mistakes and embracing the freedom from being fully forgiven.

A believer who has carried the weight of past sins may feel unworthy of God's forgiveness. However, through faith in Christ, they can receive the promise of forgiveness and walk in the freedom that comes from knowing their sins have been washed away.

Forgiving Oneself: An often-overlooked aspect of forgiveness is the need to forgive oneself. Many believers struggle to accept that they are worthy of God's love and grace, even after repenting and receiving forgiveness. Canceling the Hellbound ticket requires believers to release themselves from self-condemnation and embrace the truth that God forgives and loves them.

Believers who struggle with self-worth may continue to punish themselves for past sins, even after receiving God's forgiveness. To cancel the Hellbound ticket, they must learn to forgive themselves and trust in the sufficiency of God's grace.

Walking in Freedom: Freedom in Christ is not just about being forgiven for past sins, it is about living in the fullness of God's grace and purpose. Walking in freedom means rejecting the bondage of sin and embracing a life of holiness, joy, and purpose.

A believer who has been set free from addiction must now live in the freedom of Christ, making choices that align with their new identity as a child of God. This freedom is not simply about avoiding sin; it is about pursuing righteousness and experiencing the abundant life that God promises.

Step 5: Commit to Ongoing Spiritual Growth and Vigilance

Canceling the Hellbound ticket is not a one-time event; it is the beginning of a lifelong journey of spiritual growth and transformation. To maintain the freedom that comes from rejecting the Hellbound ticket, believers must commit to ongoing spiritual growth, vigilance, and accountability.

Pursue Holiness: Living a life of holiness is a continual process of aligning our hearts, minds, and actions with God's word. This involves daily surrender to the Holy Spirit and a commitment to obedience to God's commands.

A believer who has repented from sinful behaviors must now pursue holiness by engaging in spiritual disciplines such as prayer, Bible study, and fellowship with other believers. This ongoing commitment to spiritual growth helps to protect against future deception and temptation.

Remain Vigilant: The enemy does not give up easily. Even after canceling the Hellbound ticket, believers must remain vigilant against future attacks and temptations. This requires awareness of potential weaknesses and relying on God's strength to resist temptation.

A believer who has overcome a particular sin may face future temptations that seek to draw them back into old habits. Remaining vigilant through prayer, accountability, and reliance on God's word helps to guard against falling back into deception.

Seek Accountability: Walking in freedom is easier when believers surround themselves with a community of faith that provides support, encouragement, and accountability. Trusted friends or mentors who can speak truth into our lives and hold us accountable for our actions is essential for maintaining spiritual health.

A believer who has repented from a destructive lifestyle may benefit from joining a small group or accountability partnership where they can share their struggles and receive prayer and encouragement. This community helps to reinforce their commitment to living in freedom.

Canceling the Hellbound ticket requires a proactive and intentional approach to spiritual growth, repentance, and transformation. By acknowledging the need for repentance, engaging in genuine repentance, renouncing the enemy's lies, embracing forgiveness, and committing to ongoing spiritual growth, believers can reject the ticket that leads to spiritual death and reclaim their identity in Christ.

Prayer Points and Strategies for Overcoming Spiritual Traps

After understanding the steps necessary to reject and cancel the Hellbound ticket, believers must be equipped with specific tools and strategies to maintain spiritual freedom and avoid future traps set by the enemy. Prayer is one of the most powerful weapons in this battle, as it enables believers to connect with God, access divine strength, and gain wisdom to overcome challenges. In this section, we will discuss key prayer points and strategies for overcoming spiritual traps, providing a foundation for continuous growth and victory.

The Power of Prayer in Spiritual Warfare

Prayer is not only a means of communication with God but also an essential tool in spiritual warfare. Through prayer, believers can tap into the power of God to break free from the enemy's strongholds, seek protection from future attacks, and receive guidance on navigating spiritual traps.

Ephesians 6:18 encourages believers to "pray in the Spirit on all occasions with all kinds of prayers and requests. With this in mind, be alert and always keep on praying for all the Lord's people." This passage emphasizes the importance of constant prayer, alertness, and perseverance in spiritual warfare.

Prayer serves as both a defensive and offensive tool. It protects us from falling into temptation and spiritual traps, and it also empowers us to take authority over the enemy's schemes. Below, we will outline prayer points that specifically target common spiritual traps and provide strategies for overcoming them.

Prayer for Discernment and Wisdom

One of the most effective strategies for avoiding spiritual traps is to cultivate discernment. Discernment is the ability to distinguish between truth and deception, and it is essential for recognizing the enemy's subtle tactics. The enemy often uses confusion and doubt to lead believers astray, so it is important to seek God's wisdom to navigate these challenges.

James 1:5 states, "If any of you lacks wisdom, let him ask of God, who gives to all liberally and without reproach, and it will be given to him." This promise assures us that God is willing to grant wisdom to those who seek it.

Prayer Point:
"Father, I ask for Your wisdom and discernment in every area of my life. Help me to recognize the traps set by the enemy and to avoid falling into deception. Grant me clarity of mind and heart, so that I may always walk in Your truth and make decisions that honor You. In Jesus' name, Amen."

Strategy: Seeking God's Word

The word of God is the primary source of wisdom and discernment. By regularly studying Scripture, believers can arm themselves with the truth needed to resist deception. When faced with decisions or situations that may lead to spiritual traps, it is crucial to consult the Word of God for guidance.

Psalm 119:105 reminds us, "Your word is a lamp to my feet and a light to my path." This verse highlights the importance of God's word in providing direction and clarity in times of uncertainty.

Commit to reading and meditating on Scripture daily. When faced with difficult decisions or unclear situations, ask yourself, "What does the Bible say about this?" Seek counsel from spiritual leaders or mentors who can help you interpret and apply Scripture to your life.

Prayer for Protection from Temptation

The enemy often uses temptation as a spiritual trap to lure believers into sin. Temptation may come in the form of desires, distractions, or pressures that seem appealing but ultimately lead to spiritual downfall. Jesus Himself taught His disciples to pray for protection from temptation, knowing its potential to lead to sin.

Matthew 6:13 says, "And lead us not into temptation, but deliver us from the evil one." This prayer acknowledges the need for God's help in avoiding situations that could cause us to stumble.

Prayer Point:
"Lord, protect me from the temptations of the enemy. Help me to recognize and resist anything that seeks to draw me away from Your path. Strengthen my resolve to stand firm in my faith, even when faced with pressure, and guide me to make choices that align with Your will. In Jesus' name, Amen."

Strategy: Accountability and Boundaries

One of the most effective ways to avoid falling into temptation is to establish accountability and set clear boundaries. Accountability involves surrounding yourself with trusted individuals who can provide guidance, support, and encouragement in your spiritual journey. Setting boundaries ensures that you remain vigilant and avoid situations where temptation may be overwhelming.

Proverbs 27:17 says, "As iron sharpens iron, so a man sharpens the countenance of his friend." Accountability strengthens believers, helping them stay focused and committed to their spiritual goals.

Identify a mentor or accountability partner with whom you can share your struggles and victories. Establish clear boundaries in areas where you may be vulnerable to temptation, whether it be relationships, media consumption, or personal habits.

Prayer for Strength to Overcome Weakness

Spiritual traps often exploit areas of weakness in our lives, whether physical, emotional, or spiritual. When we are weary, discouraged, or lacking in faith, the enemy seizes these moments to intensify his attacks. Prayer for strength is vital in overcoming spiritual traps, as it invites God's power to operate in our lives, especially in moments of vulnerability.

Isaiah 40:29-31 offers comfort, stating, "He gives power to the weak, and to those who have no might He increases strength. Even the youths shall faint and be weary, and the young men shall utterly fall, but those who wait on the Lord shall renew their strength; they shall mount up with wings like eagles, they shall run and not be weary, they shall walk and not faint."

Prayer Point:
"Lord, I confess my weakness before You and ask for Your strength to overcome it. When I am tired or discouraged, renew my spirit and help me stand firm in the face of adversity. Empower me to rise above every challenge and to trust in Your power, even in my weakest moments. In Jesus' name, Amen."

Strategy: Rest and Renewal

Overcoming weakness requires rest and renewal, both physically and spiritually. When believers neglect self-care or push themselves beyond their limits, they may become more vulnerable to spiritual traps. It is essential to prioritize times of rest and refreshment to maintain spiritual vitality.

Mark 6:31 shows Jesus encouraging His disciples to rest, saying, "Come aside by yourselves to a deserted place and rest a while." Jesus recognized the importance of rest in maintaining strength for ministry.

Schedule regular times for rest and spiritual renewal. This may include taking breaks from work, engaging in worship, attending a retreat, or spending time in nature. Allow yourself to recharge so that you can approach spiritual warfare with a renewed sense of strength and focus.

Prayer for Deliverance from Bondage

Spiritual traps can sometimes lead to deeper forms of bondage, such as addiction, unforgiveness, or destructive habits. In these cases, believers may feel trapped or powerless to break free. Prayer for deliverance invites God's intervention to break the chains of bondage and restore freedom in Christ.

Psalm 107:14 proclaims, "He brought them out of darkness and the shadow of death, and broke their chains in pieces." This verse is a powerful reminder of God's ability to deliver His people from any form of bondage.

Prayer Point:
"Father, I ask for Your deliverance from any bondage that has taken hold of my life. Break every chain that keeps me bound, and set me free to walk in the freedom that Christ has secured for me. I declare victory over every stronghold in my life, and I trust in Your power to bring about total freedom. In Jesus' name, Amen."

Strategy: Confession and Renunciation

To experience deliverance from bondage, believers must be willing to confess their struggles and renounce the behaviors or mindsets that keep them bound. Confession involves acknowledging the problem before God and trusted individuals, while renunciation is the deliberate rejection of sin and its influence.

James 5:16 says, "Confess your trespasses to one another, and pray for one another, that you may be healed. The effective, fervent prayer of a righteous man avails much." Confession and prayer bring healing and restoration, creating an environment where deliverance can take place.

Identify any areas of bondage in your life and bring them to God in prayer. If necessary, seek counsel from a pastor or mentor who can pray with you and offer support. Renounce the power of the enemy over your life and declare your intention to walk in freedom.

Prayer for a Renewed Mind

The battlefield for spiritual traps often begins in the mind. Negative thoughts, doubts, and lies from the enemy can lead believers into traps of fear, insecurity, and disobedience. Praying for a renewed mind is essential to overcoming these mental traps and aligning our thoughts with God's truth.

Romans 12:2 instructs, "And do not be conformed to this world, but be transformed by the renewing of your mind, that you may prove what is that good and acceptable and perfect will of God." A renewed mind allows believers to discern God's will and resist the enemy's lies.

Prayer Point:
"Lord, renew my mind and transform my thinking according to Your Word. Remove any thoughts that do not align with Your truth, and replace them with thoughts of faith, hope, and righteousness. Help me to take every thought captive and make it obedient to Christ. In Jesus' name, Amen."

Strategy: Meditation on God's Word

Renewing the mind requires regular meditation on God's word.

Meditation allows believers to internalize Scripture, making it a guiding force in their thoughts, decisions, and actions. When the mind is filled with God's truth, it becomes more resilient to the enemy's lies.

Joshua 1:8 says, "This Book of the Law shall not depart from your mouth, but you shall meditate in it day and night, that you may observe to do according to all that is written in it. For then you will make your way prosperous, and then you will have good success."

Choose a verse or passage of Scripture to meditate on each day. Reflect on its meaning and application in your life. Allow God's word to shape your thinking and guide your decisions, particularly in areas where you are vulnerable to spiritual traps.

Overcoming spiritual traps requires a combination of prayer, discernment, and practical strategies that align with God's word. By engaging in targeted prayer points and adopting the strategies outlined above, believers can strengthen their spiritual defenses and avoid falling into the enemy's traps. Through the power of prayer and a commitment to spiritual growth, the Hellbound ticket can be canceled, and believers can walk in the freedom and victory that Christ has secured.

CHAPTER SIX

THE POWER OF COVENANT AND DIVINE INTERVENTION

Exploring God's Covenant of Mercy

T hroughout Scripture, one of the most profound themes we encounter is the covenant relationship between God and His people. A covenant is a sacred agreement, an unbreakable promise between two parties, and in the case of God, it is a divine assurance of His faithfulness, mercy, and love. Understanding God's covenant of mercy is crucial in recognizing the lengths to which God goes to redeem, restore, and protect His people. His covenantal promises are the bedrock of our faith and the foundation upon which we can stand when we face spiritual attacks, deception, and the threat of the Hellbound ticket.

In this chapter, we will explore the nature of God's covenant of mercy, examining its origins, purpose, and how it manifests in our lives today. By grasping the depth of this covenant, believers can experience a renewed sense of trust in God's faithfulness and divine intervention in moments of spiritual warfare.

The Nature of God's Covenant of Mercy

A covenant in the biblical sense is more than just a contractual agreement; it is a binding relationship established by God with His people, often sealed with promises of protection, provision, and mercy. God's covenant of mercy is a demonstration of His unrelenting love and His desire to forgive and restore those who have gone astray.

From the earliest accounts in Scripture, God's covenants have been marked by His mercy. Even when humanity sinned and distanced itself from God, His covenant promises reflected His desire to restore and heal that relationship. The concept of mercy is integral to these covenants because mercy allows for grace, forgiveness, and restoration in the face of human failure.

The Covenant with Noah: One of the earliest expressions of God's covenant of mercy is seen in His agreement with Noah. After the flood, which was a judgment on the earth for its wickedness, God made a promise to Noah and to all living creatures that He would never again destroy the earth by flood. This covenant was sealed with the sign of a rainbow (Genesis 9:12-17). Despite humanity's rebellion, God's mercy prevailed, and He offered a fresh start, showcasing His compassion and grace.

Genesis 9:16: "The rainbow shall be in the cloud, and I will look on it to remember the everlasting covenant between God and every living creature of all flesh that is on the earth." This covenant is a lasting reminder of God's mercy toward His creation, even in the face of judgment.

The Covenant with Abraham: God's covenant with Abraham is another powerful example of His mercy. In this covenant, God promised Abraham that his descendants would become a great nation and that through them, all the families of the earth would be blessed (Genesis 12:1-3). Despite Abraham's moments of doubt and the moral failings of his descendants, God's covenant remained unshaken because it was based on His mercy and faithfulness, not human performance.

Genesis 17:7: "And I will establish My covenant between Me and you and your descendants after you in their generations, for an everlasting covenant, to be God to you and your descendants after you." This covenant reveals the unrelenting mercy of God, extending beyond Abraham to his descendants, ensuring that they would remain under His care despite their imperfections.

The Mosaic Covenant: When God established the Mosaic covenant with the Israelites at Mount Sinai, He gave them the Law, which included moral, civil, and ceremonial instructions for living in a way that reflected His holiness. Yet, God's mercy was evident even in the giving of the Law, for He knew the people would struggle to keep it perfectly. That is why He instituted sacrifices as a means of atoning for sin, allowing His people to continually receive His mercy and forgiveness.

Exodus 34:6-7: "The Lord, the Lord God, merciful and gracious, longsuffering, and abounding in goodness and truth, keeping mercy for thousands, forgiving iniquity and transgression and sin, by no means clearing the guilty." This description of God's character established His desire to show mercy even when humanity fails to meet His standards.

Mercy in the New Covenant: The Ultimate Expression

While the covenants of the Old Testament reveal God's merciful nature, it is in the New Covenant, established through the life, death, and resurrection of Jesus Christ, that we see the ultimate expression of God's mercy. The New Covenant is built on better promises and offers a way for humanity to be reconciled to God permanently, not through the repeated sacrifices of animals, but through the once-for-all sacrifice of Christ.

The Fulfillment of God's Promise: The New Covenant fulfills the promises made in the Old Testament, particularly the covenant made with Abraham. Jesus is the promised seed through whom all nations would be blessed (Galatians 3:16). His death on the cross is the greatest act of mercy in human history, as it provided a means for forgiveness, redemption, and eternal life for all who believe.

Luke 22:20: "Likewise He also took the cup after supper, saying, 'This cup is the new covenant in My blood, which is shed for you.'" Jesus' blood sealed the New Covenant, ensuring that mercy is available to all who call on His name.

Mercy for All Humanity: The New Covenant extends God's mercy to all humanity, breaking down the barriers between Jews and Gentiles and inviting everyone into a relationship with God. No longer is access to God limited by ethnicity, nationality, or adherence to the Law. Instead, faith in Christ is the basis for receiving God's mercy.

Ephesians 2:4-5: "But God, who is rich in mercy, because of His great love with which He loved us, even when we were dead in trespasses, made us alive together with Christ (by grace you have been saved)." This passage signifies the richness of God's mercy, which reaches out to those who were spiritually dead and offers them new life in Christ.

Forgiveness and Restoration: Through the New Covenant, forgiveness is no longer dependent on the annual sacrifices of the Old Testament. Instead, believers can experience immediate forgiveness and restoration through repentance and faith in Christ. This mercy is not limited by the severity of the sin, as God's grace abounds even in the worst of circumstances.

Hebrews 8:12: "For I will be merciful to their unrighteousness, and their sins and their lawless deeds I will remember no more." This promise of mercy assures believers that their past mistakes do not define them, and God's forgiveness is complete and final.

Living in the Covenant of Mercy

Understanding the covenant of mercy is one thing, but living in it requires a conscious effort to embrace God's promises and walk in the freedom that His mercy provides. The covenant of mercy is not a license to continue in sin but an invitation to live in alignment with God's will, knowing that His mercy is always available when we fall short. Below are several ways believers can live in the covenant of mercy:

Embrace God's Grace Daily: The New Covenant is built on grace, not human effort. While obedience is important, believers must recognize that their relationship with God is based on His grace and mercy, not their ability to follow rules perfectly.

Ephesians 2:8-9: "For by grace you have been saved through faith, and that not of yourselves; it is the gift of God, not of works, lest anyone should boast." This verse reminds us that God's mercy is not something we can earn, it is a gift freely given to all who believe.

Extend Mercy to Others: As recipients of God's mercy, believers are called to extend that same mercy to others. This includes forgiving those who have wronged us, showing compassion to those in need, and offering grace to those who struggle.

Matthew 5:7: "Blessed are the merciful, for they shall obtain mercy." Jesus emphasized the importance of showing mercy to others as a reflection of the mercy we have received from God.

Confess and Repent Regularly: While God's mercy is abundant, it is important for believers to maintain a lifestyle of repentance and humility. Confessing sins and seeking God's forgiveness allows believers to remain in a place of mercy, free from the burden of guilt and shame.

1 John 1:9: "If we confess our sins, He is faithful and just to forgive us our sins and to cleanse us from all unrighteousness." This ongoing practice of confession keeps believers in alignment with God's mercy and ensures that they remain in right relationship with Him.

Walk in Confidence and Freedom: God's covenant of mercy provides believers with the assurance that they are loved, forgiven, and accepted. This confidence allows believers to live free from fear, knowing that God's mercy covers their past, present, and future.

Romans 8:1: "There is therefore now no condemnation to those who are in Christ Jesus, who do not walk according to the flesh, but according to the Spirit." This verse is a powerful reminder that the covenant of mercy removes all condemnation, enabling believers to live in the freedom that Christ provides.

Divine Intervention Through the Covenant of Mercy

One of the most powerful aspects of God's covenant of mercy is His willingness to intervene in the lives of His people. Divine intervention refers to God stepping into human circumstances to bring about His will, often rescuing, protecting, or providing for His people in ways that go beyond natural explanation. Throughout the Bible, we see numerous examples of divine intervention, all rooted in God's covenant of mercy.

Deliverance from Enemies: In the Old Testament, God often intervened to deliver His people from their enemies as part of His covenant promises. Whether it was the Israelites' escape from Egypt or David's victory over Goliath, these acts of divine intervention were expressions of God's mercy and His commitment to protect His people.

Psalm 18:17: "He delivered me from my strong enemy, from those who hated me, for they were too strong for me." This verse captures the essence of divine intervention, where God steps in to rescue His people from overwhelming odds.

Provision in Times of Need: Divine intervention is also evident in God's provision for His people during times of need. Whether it was manna from heaven for the Israelites in the wilderness or Jesus multiplying loaves and fish to feed thousands, God's mercy extended to meeting the physical needs of His people.

Philippians 4:19: "And my God shall supply all your need

according to His riches in glory by Christ Jesus." This promise assures believers that God's mercy extends to every area of life, including provision for daily needs.

Healing and Restoration: Another form of divine intervention is seen in God's healing and restoration. Throughout the Gospels, Jesus healed the sick, raised the dead, and restored the broken, all as a demonstration of God's mercy. These acts of intervention continue today, as believers pray for healing and experience God's miraculous touch.

Psalm 103:3-4: "Who forgives all your iniquities, who heals all your diseases, who redeems your life from destruction, who crowns you with lovingkindness and tender mercies." This passage reveals God's desire to heal and restore His people, both physically and spiritually, as part of His covenant of mercy.

Guidance and Direction: Divine intervention is not limited to dramatic miracles; it also includes the quiet, yet profound, guidance that God provides through His Holy Spirit. As part of His covenant of mercy, God promises to lead His people in the right direction, protecting them from spiritual traps and guiding them toward His will.

Proverbs 3:5-6: "Trust in the Lord with all your heart, and lean not on your own understanding; in all your ways acknowledge Him, and He shall direct your paths." This promise of guidance is a reflection of God's covenant faithfulness, ensuring that believers are never left to navigate life's challenges on their own.

God's covenant of mercy is one of the most powerful expressions of His love and faithfulness toward humanity. Through this covenant, believers can experience forgiveness, restoration, and divine intervention in every area of life. Whether it is deliverance from enemies, provision in times of need, or guidance through life's challenges, God's mercy is a constant source of hope and strength. By living in the reality of this covenant, believers can walk in confidence, knowing that God's promises are unbreakable and His love is unfailing.

How to Invoke God's Covenant in Times of Trouble

In the Christian journey, every believer will inevitably face times of trouble, whether in the form of personal challenges, spiritual warfare, or unexpected trials. During such times, understanding how to invoke God's covenant of mercy and protection becomes crucial. God's covenant is not merely a theological concept but a practical, life-changing promise that believers can rely on in their daily lives.

A covenant, in its biblical context, is an unbreakable promise between God and His people. God's covenants throughout Scripture, especially the New Covenant established through Jesus Christ, assure us that He will remain faithful even when we face difficulty. In times of trouble, invoking God's covenant is about calling upon the promises He has made and trusting in His character as a covenant-keeping God.

God's Covenant Is Based on His Faithfulness, Not Our Performance: One of the most encouraging aspects of God's covenant is that it is rooted in His faithfulness, not in our ability to earn or deserve His help. Even when we are weak, failing, or struggling, God's covenant remains intact because He has bound Himself to His promises.

2 Timothy 2:13 reminds us, "If we are faithless, He remains faithful; He cannot deny Himself." This passage underscores the fact that God's covenant is based on His nature. His faithfulness is unchanging, which is why we can confidently call on Him in times of need.

The Covenant Provides Protection and Deliverance: Throughout Scripture, we see God's covenant used as a means of protection and deliverance for His people. From Noah's safety during the flood to the Israelites' deliverance from Egypt, God's covenant promises ensured their survival and victory.

Psalm 91:4: "He shall cover you with His feathers, and under His wings you shall take refuge; His truth shall be your shield and buckler." This image of divine protection reflects the security that comes from living under God's covenant.

In times of trouble, invoking God's covenant means calling upon these divine promises and asking God to intervene based on the eternal bond He has established with us.

Step 1: Remember and Declare God's Covenant Promises

The first step in invoking God's covenant in times of trouble is to remember and declare His promises. God has provided numerous assurances of His love, protection, guidance, and deliverance throughout the Bible. These promises are foundational to the covenant, and they serve as a lifeline when we are in need.

Meditate on God's Promises: When trouble arises, it's easy to become overwhelmed by fear, anxiety, or doubt. However, Scripture teaches that we should not fix our eyes on our problems but on God's promises. Meditating on His word reminds us of His covenant and helps us shift our focus from our circumstances to His faithfulness.

Isaiah 26:3: "You will keep him in perfect peace, whose mind is stayed on You, because he trusts in You." Meditating on God's promises allows believers to experience peace even in the midst of trials.

If you are facing financial difficulties, meditate on promises like Philippians 4:19, "And my God shall supply all your need according to His riches in glory by Christ Jesus." Declare that God, who has covenanted to provide for His children, will meet your needs.

Declare God's Promises in Prayer: After meditating on God's promises, the next step is to declare them in prayer. Speaking the promises aloud serves as a form of spiritual warfare, reminding ourselves and the enemy that we belong to God and His Word stands forever.

Isaiah 55:11: "So shall My word be that goes forth from My mouth; it shall not return to Me void, but it shall accomplish what I please, and it shall prosper in the thing for which I sent it." Declaring God's promises aligns our hearts with His truth and releases the power of His Word into our situation.

Prayer Point:
"Lord, I thank You for Your covenant promises. Your Word declares that You are my refuge and strength, a very present help in trouble. I declare that You are with me in this situation, and I stand on Your promises of deliverance, protection, and provision. Your covenant is unbreakable, and I trust in Your faithfulness. In Jesus' name, Amen."

Step 2: Call on God's Name and His Covenant Faithfulness

In times of trouble, calling on God's name is a powerful way to invoke His covenant. Throughout Scripture, the names of God reveal His character and His covenant relationship with His people. Calling on His name in prayer allows us to focus on His attributes and trust in His intervention.

Invoke the Name of God as a Covenant-Keeper: God's covenant names reveal aspects of His faithfulness and His willingness to intervene on behalf of His people. In the Old Testament, God was often referred to by specific names that reflected His covenant with Israel. These names still hold power for believers today because they reveal eternal truths about God's nature.

Jehovah Jireh (The Lord Will Provide) –
Genesis 22:14: When facing financial need, invoke God's name as Jehovah Jireh, declaring that He is your provider according to His covenant promises.

Jehovah Rapha (The Lord Who Heals) Exodus 15:26: If you are battling sickness, call upon God as Jehovah Rapha, standing on His promise of healing.

Jehovah Shalom (The Lord Is Peace) – Judges 6:24: When anxiety or fear threatens to overwhelm you, declare that Jehovah Shalom is with you, bringing peace that surpasses understanding.

If you are experiencing fear and uncertainty, you can pray:
"Jehovah Shalom, I call on Your name today. You are the God of peace, and I declare that Your peace is covering my heart and mind. In the midst of this storm, I trust in Your covenant to bring calm and assurance. You are with me, and I will not fear. Amen."

Appeal to God's Covenant Faithfulness: Invoking God's covenant in times of trouble also means reminding Him of His covenant faithfulness. This is not because God forgets His promises, but because calling on His faithfulness strengthens our faith and deepens our trust in His ability to act.

Nehemiah 1:5: "And I said: 'I pray, Lord God of heaven, O great and awesome God, You who keep Your covenant and mercy with those who love You and observe Your commandments.'" Nehemiah invoked God's covenant faithfulness when interceding for the people of Israel, trusting that God's promises would not fail.

Prayer Point:
"Lord, I appeal to Your faithfulness. You are a covenant-keeping God, and You have promised never to leave me nor forsake me. I call on Your faithfulness in this time of trouble, trusting that You will make a way where there seems to be no way. Your covenant stands firm, and I stand on Your Word. In Jesus' name, Amen."

Step 3: Offer Prayers of Repentance and Surrender

Another essential aspect of invoking God's covenant in times of trouble is ensuring that there is no sin or disobedience blocking the flow of God's blessings. While God's covenant is based on His grace and mercy, sin can hinder our ability to fully experience the benefits of that covenant. Repentance and surrender are key to aligning ourselves with God's will and opening the door for His intervention.

Repentance Restores Covenant Relationship: When believers stray from God's commandments or live in disobedience, it does not mean that God's covenant is broken, but it can create a barrier between us and the full expression of His blessings. Through repentance, believers can restore their covenant relationship with God and invite His mercy to work in their lives.

2 Chronicles 7:14: "If My people who are called by My name will humble themselves, and pray and seek My face, and turn from their wicked ways, then I will hear from heaven, and will forgive their sin and heal their land." This verse emphasizes the importance of repentance in invoking God's covenant blessings.

If you are facing difficulty due to personal sin or disobedience, you can pray:
"Lord, I come before You in repentance. I acknowledge that I have strayed from Your ways, and I ask for Your forgiveness. Cleanse me from all unrighteousness and restore my covenant relationship with You. I surrender my heart and my will to You, trusting in Your mercy and grace. In Jesus' name, Amen."

Surrender to God's Plan and Purpose: Invoking God's covenant also involves surrendering our plans, desires, and outcomes to Him. Sometimes, the trouble we face is an opportunity for God to work in ways that we cannot see or understand. By surrendering to His will, we align ourselves with His greater purposes, trusting that He will work all things for our good.

Romans 8:28: "And we know that all things work together for good to those who love God, to those who are the called according to His purpose." Surrendering to God's plan means trusting that His covenant promises will lead to a good outcome, even if the process is difficult.

Prayer Point:
"Lord, I surrender this situation to You. I trust in Your covenant

promises, and I believe that You are working all things together for my good. Even when I don't understand what is happening, I choose to trust in Your plan and Your purpose. Have Your way in my life, and let Your will be done. In Jesus' name, Amen."

Step 4: Stand Firm in Faith and Perseverance

Invoking God's covenant in times of trouble requires standing firm in faith and perseverance. While God's covenant promises are sure, the enemy will often try to shake our faith or cause us to doubt that God will come through. Persevering in faith means holding on to God's word, even when circumstances seem to contradict His promises.

Stand on God's Promises Without Wavering: Faith is the key to accessing the blessings of God's covenant. When we pray and invoke His promises, we must stand firm in the belief that God will answer. This does not mean that every situation will resolve immediately, but it does mean that we trust God's timing and His ability to bring about His will.

Hebrews 10:23: "Let us hold fast the confession of our hope without wavering, for He who promised is faithful." This verse encourages believers to remain steadfast in their faith, knowing that God's covenant promises are reliable.

If you are facing prolonged trials, you can pray:
    "Lord, I stand firm on Your promises today. I will not waver in my faith, even when I don't see immediate results. I know that You are faithful, and I trust in Your covenant to bring about deliverance in Your perfect time. Strengthen my faith and help me to persevere. In Jesus' name, Amen."

Persevere Through Prayer and Worship: One of the most powerful ways to stand firm in faith is through continual prayer and worship. Worship shifts our focus from the problem to the greatness of God, reminding us of His ability to intervene. Prayer keeps us connected to God's promises and allows us to receive His strength and encouragement.

1 Thessalonians 5:17: "Pray without ceasing." This command encourages believers to remain in constant communication with God, especially during times of trouble. Persevering in prayer keeps our hearts aligned with God's will and helps us navigate challenges with grace.

Set aside dedicated time each day for prayer and worship, even in the midst of trials. Surround yourself with worship music, Scripture readings, and prayer time that refocuses your heart on God's covenant promises.

Invoking God's covenant in times of trouble is a powerful spiritual practice that allows believers to access His promises of protection, provision, deliverance, and peace. By remembering and declaring God's promises, calling on His name, repenting and surrendering, and standing firm in faith, believers can experience divine intervention and breakthrough. God's covenant is unbreakable, and His mercy is unfailing, giving every believer the assurance that He will remain faithful in every season of life.

CHAPTER SEVEN

TESTIMONIES OF DELIVERANCE

Personal Stories of People Who
Were Delivered by God's Covenant

One of the most powerful ways to illustrate the reality and effectiveness of God's covenant is through testimonies of deliverance. Testimonies are more than just stories of victory, they are tangible evidence of God's intervention, His mercy, and His faithfulness in the lives of His people. When we hear the accounts of others who have been delivered from bondage, spiritual traps, and impossible situations, it strengthens our faith and reminds us of the unbreakable promises we have in Christ.

These testimonies highlight the power of God's covenant to bring about freedom from spiritual and physical oppression, protection in times of danger, and restoration of broken lives. They serve as reminders that the same God who delivered the people of Israel from Egypt and rescued Daniel from the lion's den is still at work today, delivering His people from the schemes of the enemy and turning their trials into triumphs.

The Power of Testimonies

Testimonies have always played an important role in the life of the believer. In the Old Testament, God commanded the Israelites to remember and retell the stories of His deliverance so that future generations would know and trust in His faithfulness. In the New Testament, testimonies of healing, salvation, and deliverance are recorded as a testament to the power of Jesus' ministry.

Revelation 12:11 speaks to the power of testimonies in spiritual warfare, stating: "And they overcame him by the blood of the Lamb and by the word of their testimony, and they did not love their lives to the death." This place emphasizes that the sharing of testimonies is a vital part of overcoming the enemy. The recounting of God's intervention strengthens the faith of the listener and reminds the believer of the victory secured through Christ.

Testimonies also serve as a form of spiritual warfare because they dismantle the lies of the enemy. The enemy often seeks to convince us that we are alone in our struggles, that our situation is beyond hope, or that God is not concerned with our deliverance. When we hear the testimonies of others who have been set free, these lies are exposed, and we are reminded that God is still in the business of saving, healing, and delivering.

Testimony 1: Deliverance from Addiction

One of the most common spiritual traps is addiction, whether it be to substances, behaviors, or destructive habits. Many people feel trapped in cycles of addiction, believing that they are powerless to break free. However, God's covenant of mercy and deliverance extends even to the darkest corners of addiction. The following testimony is an example of how invoking God's covenant promises can bring freedom and restoration.

Sarah's Story:
Sarah had struggled with alcohol addiction for over a decade. What started as casual drinking with friends quickly escalated

into a daily habit that she couldn't control. Over the years, her addiction led to the loss of relationships, jobs, and her sense of self-worth. Sarah knew she needed help but felt powerless to change. She had tried multiple rehab programs and had even attended church sporadically, but nothing seemed to work. Deep down, she believed that God was angry with her and that she didn't deserve His help.

One day, during a particularly low moment, Sarah stumbled upon a Bible that had been sitting on her shelf for years. She began reading the story of the Prodigal Son in Luke 15, and for the first time, she saw herself in the story. She realized that just as the father in the story welcomed his wayward son with open arms, God was ready to welcome her back, no matter how far she had fallen. Moved to tears, Sarah prayed for the first time in years, asking God to deliver her from her addiction and restore her life.

That moment marked the beginning of Sarah's journey to deliverance. She began attending a local church and was connected with a small group of believers who prayed with her regularly. One of the members shared with Sarah about the power of God's covenant promises and encouraged her to declare those promises over her life. Sarah clung to verses like Isaiah 41:10, which says, "Fear not, for I am with you; be not dismayed, for I am your God. I will strengthen you, yes, I will help you, I will uphold you with My righteous right hand."

Over the course of several months, Sarah saw God's deliverance unfold in her life. The cravings that had once controlled her began to diminish, and she found strength in prayer and community. Today, Sarah is completely free from her addiction and uses her testimony to encourage others who are struggling with similar battles. She often shares how invoking God's covenant of mercy, through prayer, Scripture, and fellowship, transformed her life.

Sarah's story highlights the power of God's covenant to break the chains of addiction. No matter how deep the bondage, God's mercy is greater, and His deliverance is available to all who seek it. Her testimony also illustrates the importance of community, prayer, and the declaration of God's promises in overcoming spiritual traps.

Testimony 2: Protection from Harm

God's covenant promises include not only deliverance from sin but also protection from physical harm. Throughout Scripture, we see countless examples of God protecting His people in times of danger, whether it be Daniel in the lion's den or Shadrach, Meshach, and Abednego in the fiery furnace. The following testimony demonstrates how invoking God's covenant of protection can bring deliverance in moments of life-threatening danger.

John's Story:
John was a missionary serving in a remote part of Africa when his village came under attack by a violent rebel group. The group was known for terrorizing the region, and many people in John's village had fled in fear for their lives. However, John and a few other believers decided to stay and pray, trusting that God would protect them. As the sound of gunfire and shouting drew closer, John and his group gathered in a small house and began to pray fervently, invoking Psalm 91, which speaks of God's protection and deliverance.

They declared verses like Psalm 91:7, which says, "A thousand may fall at your side, and ten thousand at your right hand, but it shall not come near you." They asked God to cover them with His wings and to protect them from the violence that surrounded them. Despite the fear that gripped their hearts, they continued to pray, standing on the covenant promise that God is their refuge and fortress.

Miraculously, the rebel group passed through the village without harming John or any believers. Though the group had terrorized other nearby towns, burning homes and taking lives, John's group was completely untouched. They later learned that other villagers had fled to the forest and survived, confirming that God's hand of protection had been over the entire village.

John's testimony is a powerful reminder of God's covenant of protection. In times of danger, invoking God's promises and trusting in His ability to protect can lead to miraculous deliverance. Psalm 91 is often referred to as the "Covenant of Protection," and John's experience is a testament to the power of praying and declaring God's Word in times of peril.

Testimony 3: Restoration of a Broken Family

God's covenant is not only about protection and deliverance from physical harm or addiction; it also includes the restoration of broken relationships. Many families experience pain, division, and conflict, and it can sometimes feel as though reconciliation is impossible. However, God's covenant of mercy extends to healing fractured relationships and restoring what has been lost.

Lydia's Story:
Lydia had been estranged from her daughter, Emily, for over five years. Their relationship had always been tumultuous, but after a particularly heated argument, Emily left home and refused to speak to her mother. The pain of the separation weighed heavily on Lydia, and she often cried out to God, asking for reconciliation. However, as the years passed, she began to lose hope that her relationship with Emily could ever be restored.

One day, during a church service, Lydia felt a strong prompting from the Holy Spirit to stand on God's covenant promises for her family. She remembered Jeremiah 31:16-17, which says, "'Refrain your voice from weeping, and your eyes from tears; for your work shall be rewarded,' says the Lord, 'And they shall come back from the land of the enemy. There is hope in your future,' says the Lord, 'That your children shall come back to their own border.'" Lydia took this promise to heart and began to pray for Emily's return, declaring that God would heal their relationship.

Over the next few months, Lydia continued to pray, invoking God's covenant of mercy and trusting that He was working behind the scenes. One evening, out of the blue, Lydia received a phone call from Emily. With tears in her voice, Emily apologized for the years of silence and expressed a desire to reconnect. Over the next several months, Lydia and Emily worked through their issues and began to rebuild their relationship. Today, they are closer than ever, and Lydia often shares her testimony of how God restored her family through His covenant promises.

Lydia's testimony shows that no relationship is beyond the reach of God's mercy. Whether it's a broken family, a strained friendship, or a marriage on the brink of collapse, God's restoration covenant is available to those who trust in Him. By standing on God's promises and praying for reconciliation, Lydia experienced the healing power of God's covenant in her family.

Encouragement to Live a Life Free from Spiritual Bondage

Living in a world filled with challenges, distractions, and spiritual traps can often leave believers feeling weighed down and trapped in cycles of sin and despair. However, the testimonies of deliverance we've explored in the previous section serve as powerful reminders that freedom from spiritual bondage is not only possible but available to every believer through the grace and mercy of God.

Spiritual bondage can manifest in various forms, including addiction, sin, unhealthy relationships, fear, guilt, and shame. These chains can keep believers from experiencing the fullness of life that God intended. The enemy seeks to bind us with guilt over our past, fear of the future, and distractions from our purpose. However, understanding that Jesus came to set us free is vital for embracing a life without bondage.

Jesus' Mission of Deliverance: The heart of the Gospel is found in Jesus' declaration of His mission. In Luke 4:18, Jesus proclaimed,

"The Spirit of the Lord is upon Me because He has anointed Me to preach the gospel to the poor; He has sent Me to heal the brokenhearted, to proclaim liberty to the captives and recovery of sight to the blind, to set at liberty those who are oppressed." This mission encapsulates God's desire to bring freedom and healing to all who are trapped in bondage.

The Bondage of Sin: Sin has a binding effect, ensnaring individuals and leading them down a path of destruction. Romans 6:16 reminds us, "Do you not know that to whom you present yourselves slaves to obey, you are that one's slaves whom you obey, whether of sin leading to death, or of obedience leading to righteousness?" This verse shows the importance of choosing obedience to God, which leads to freedom from sin's grip.

The Promise of Freedom: God's covenant promises freedom for His people. Galatians 5:1 declares, "Stand fast therefore in the liberty by which Christ has made us free, and do not be entangled again with a yoke of bondage." This verse encourages believers to embrace the freedom that Christ provides and to resist the temptation to return to old patterns of sin.

The Importance of Embracing Freedom

Embracing freedom from spiritual bondage requires intentional action and a willingness to walk in the truth of God's word. The path to freedom begins with understanding our identity in Christ and the power that comes from His sacrifice.

Recognizing Our Identity in Christ: Understanding who we are in Christ is foundational to living free from bondage. When we accept Jesus as our Lord and Savior, we become new creations (2 Corinthians 5:17). This new identity means that we are no longer defined by our past mistakes or sins but by the righteousness of Christ.

Ephesians 1:7 says, "In Him, we have redemption through His blood, the forgiveness of sins, according to the riches of His grace."

This verse highlights that our identity is rooted in redemption and forgiveness, not in our failures.

Claiming God's Promises: God's word is filled with promises about our freedom. Regularly meditating on and declaring these promises remind us of the truth that God has set us free.

John 8:36 says, "Therefore if the Son makes you free, you shall be free indeed." This promise assures us that freedom is not just a concept but a reality that can be experienced in our lives.

Living Out Our Freedom: Embracing freedom means actively choosing to live in accordance with God's will. This involves making decisions that align with His Word and resisting the temptation to revert to old patterns of behavior that lead to bondage.

Romans 12:2 instructs believers to "not be conformed to this world, but be transformed by the renewing of your mind, that you may prove what is that good and acceptable and perfect will of God." Renewing our minds through Scripture allows us to break free from worldly influences and align our lives with God's purposes.

Practical Steps to Maintain Spiritual Freedom

While understanding our identity and God's promises is essential, practical steps must be taken to maintain spiritual freedom. These steps can help believers handle challenges and ensure they do not fall back into bondage.

Engage in Regular Prayer: Prayer is a powerful tool for maintaining spiritual freedom. It connects us with God, strengthens our faith, and allows us to seek His guidance in difficult situations.

Philippians 4:6-7 encourages believers to "be anxious for nothing, but in everything by prayer and supplication, with thanksgiving, let your requests be made known to God; and the peace of God, which surpasses all understanding, will guard your hearts and minds through Christ Jesus." Regularly engaging in prayer helps to maintain peace and clarity in our lives.

Establish Healthy Boundaries: Setting boundaries is crucial for avoiding situations that may lead to temptation or spiritual traps. This can include distancing oneself from unhealthy relationships, limiting exposure to negative influences, or avoiding environments that trigger old habits.

Proverbs 4:23 states, "Keep your heart with all diligence, for out of it spring the issues of life." By guarding our hearts and minds, we can protect ourselves from influences that lead back to bondage.

Seek Accountability: Being part of a supportive community of believers is vital for maintaining spiritual freedom. Accountability provides encouragement, prayer, and support in moments of weakness.

Ecclesiastes 4:9-10 reminds us, "Two are better than one because they have a good reward for their labor. For if they fall, one will lift his companion." Surrounding ourselves with fellow believers who can support us helps reinforce our commitment to living in freedom.

Commit to Spiritual Growth: Regularly engaging in Bible study, attending church, and participating in spiritual growth activities deepens our understanding of God's Word and strengthens our faith.

2 Peter 3:18 encourages believers to "grow in the grace and knowledge of our Lord and Savior Jesus Christ." A commitment to spiritual growth equips us to face challenges with the knowledge and strength found in Christ.

Declare Freedom: It is essential to speak of freedom and victory over our lives. Regularly declaring God's promises can reinforce our identity in Christ and remind us of the truth that we are free.

Galatians 5:1 reminds us, "Stand fast therefore in the liberty by which Christ has made us free." Declaring this truth in prayer and worship reinforces our commitment to freedom.

Embracing a Life of Freedom

Living a life free from spiritual bondage is a continuous journey that requires intentionality, commitment, and reliance on God's strength. As believers, we must recognize that the enemy will attempt to sow seeds of doubt, fear, and temptation, but we can stand firm in our faith and claim the freedom that Christ has provided.

Embrace a Spirit of Resilience: Life will present challenges, but cultivating resilience in adversity is essential for maintaining freedom. Trusting in God's promises and relying on His strength will empower us to persevere through difficulties.

James 1:2-4 teaches us, "My brethren, count it all joy when you fall into various trials, knowing that testing your faith produces patience. But let patience have its perfect work, that you may be perfect and complete, lacking nothing." Viewing trials as opportunities for growth helps build spiritual resilience.

Stay Focused on the Truth: In a world filled with lies and distractions, staying focused on God's truth is essential. Regularly immersing ourselves in Scripture will help us discern truth from falsehood and guard against spiritual traps.

John 17:17 states, "Sanctify them by Your truth. Your word is truth." God's word is a powerful tool for maintaining clarity and focus on His promises.

Live with Hope and Expectation: Embracing a life free from bondage means living with hope and expectation for God's continued work. Expecting God to move and intervene fosters an attitude of faith and trust.

Romans 15:13: "Now may the God of hope fill you with all joy and peace in believing, that you may abound in hope by the power of the Holy Spirit." Living with hope empowers us to confidently look forward to the future, knowing God is at work.

Share Your Testimony: Sharing your story of deliverance and freedom can inspire and encourage others who may be struggling. Testimonies serve as a source of encouragement for others and reinforce our faith as we recount God's faithfulness.

Psalm 66:16: "Come and hear, all you who fear God, and I will declare what He has done for my soul." Sharing your journey can be a powerful way to invoke God's covenant and encourage others to seek their deliverance.

Living free from spiritual bondage is not just a possibility; it is God's desire for every believer. Through the power of His covenant and the strength found in Christ, we can break free from the chains that seek to bind us. The testimonies of deliverance we've explored are potent reminders of God's faithfulness and mercy.

As we embrace our identity in Christ, invoke His promises, and engage in practical steps to maintain our freedom, we position ourselves to experience the fullness of life God intends. Let us be encouraged to walk in faith, share our testimonies, and help others find their way to freedom through the unchanging covenant of mercy that God has established with His people.

CONCLUSION

Walking In Freedom And
Spiritual Authority

A s we conclude this book, it is clear that the spiritual journey is one marked by choices that determine whether we accept the "hellbound ticket" the enemy offers or the abundant life promised by God. This book has unveiled the subtle ways the enemy deceives, manipulates, and traps individuals into accepting a path of spiritual destruction. Yet, more importantly, it has revealed the unmatched power of God's covenant, His mercy, and His redemptive plan for humanity.

The message of this book is a call to awareness and action. It has shown that we must be vigilant, discerning the spiritual forces and the enemy's strategies. Sin, disobedience, and spiritual compromise are tools the enemy uses to lure people away from their God-given destiny. However, we can cancel the hellbound ticket and reclaim our spiritual authority by invoking God's covenant of mercy and embracing a life of repentance, obedience, and reliance on Christ's sacrifice.

As you close the pages of this book, you are encouraged to walk in the freedom that Christ has secured for you. Spiritual freedom is not simply about avoiding sin but about living in the fullness of God's grace, walking in purpose, and standing firm against the enemy's attacks. The choices you make every day, whether to live in alignment with God's will or to succumb to temptation, have eternal consequences.

Remember, God's promises are unshakable, His mercy is limitless, and His power to deliver is beyond measure. By seeking His guidance through prayer, immersing yourself in His word, and walking in obedience, you can live a life free from spiritual bondage and empowered by His Spirit.

The path to eternal life is open, and the power to reject the hellbound ticket lies in your hands. Embrace the grace, mercy, and freedom that are yours through Christ, and step confidently into the life of victory that God has prepared for you.

A SPECIAL CALL TO SALVATION & NEW BEGINNINGS FROM APOSTLE DR. DAVID PHILEMON

D ear Beloved,
God loves you deeply and has brought you to this moment for a reason. No matter your past, His love and forgiveness are available to you.

The Bible says in John 3:16, "For God so loved the world that He gave His one and only Son, that whoever believes in Him shall not perish but have eternal life." Jesus Christ came to save you, offering you a new life of purpose and peace.

If you're ready to accept Jesus as your Lord and Savior, pray this simple prayer:

The Salvation Prayer

"Heavenly Father, I come to You in the Name of Jesus. I acknowledge that I am a sinner in need of a Savior. I believe that Jesus Christ is Your Son, that He died for my sins, and that You raised Him from the dead. I repent of my sins and turn to You with

my
Whole heart. Jesus, I ask You to come into my life. Be my Lord and my Savior. I surrender my life to You. Fill me with Your Holy Spirit, guide me on the path of righteousness, and help me to follow Your script for my life. Thank you, Father, for saving me. In the name of Jesus. Amen."

Welcome to the Family of God!

If you have just prayed this prayer, Congratulations! You are now a child of God, and heaven is rejoicing. Your journey has begun, and we're here to support you as you grow in faith and discover God's unique plans for you.

Next Steps:
• Connect with a Bible-believing church.
• Read the Bible Daily: God's Word is your guide.
• Pray Regularly: Prayer is your lifeline to God.
• Share Your Faith: Don't keep the good news to yourself.

www.ingramcontent.com/pod-product-compliance
Lightning Source LLC
Chambersburg PA
CBHW071901020426

42331CB00010B/2617